JOSEPH

JOSEPH

A *Life* of Rejection, Resilience and Respect

JESSIE SENECA

JOSEPH
A Life of Rejection, Resilience and Respect

ISBN 978-1-886068-86-5
Library of Congress Control Number: 2014947611
Religion, Christian, Personal Growth

Published by Fruitbearer Publishing, LLC
P.O. Box 777, Georgetown, DE 19947
302.856.6649 • FAX 302.856.7742
www.fruitbearer.com • info@fruitbearer.com

Edited by Fran D. Lowe
Cover design by Kelly Vanek, Cassidy Communications, Inc.
Interior design by Jackielou Orcino

Printed in the United States of America

Dedicated

To my prayer team, you know who you are.

You have encouraged me along the way of the dusty road
from Canaan to Egypt.

You have encouraged me when I was tired,
and some of you viewed the unedited first look of Joseph.

Without you, I wouldn't be where we are today.

I say "we" because this study has been a group effort
and written with you in mind.

Meet the Author

Jessie Seneca is a national speaker, author, leadership trainer and founder of More of Him Ministries. She also works with LifeWay as a Living Proof Live City Coordinator and Northeast Simulcast Specialist. She has a passion to help women experience God's Word for themselves as she encourages you to move into a "wholehearted" lifestyle, one devoted fully to God. Jessie has written *The Secret is Out*, a Bible study from the book of Colossians, and her personal journey through life's detours and pit stops, *Road Trip*. Her desire is for you to see God's big picture in your life and encourage you to live a more purposeful life as you search the scripture and apply it to your every day journey.

Jessie and her husband, John live in Bethlehem, Pennsylvania and have two adult daughters, Lauren and Sarah. She enjoys walking her dogs, Bella and Murphy, laughing with her family and spending time with friends.

Table of Contents

Facilitator Guide

Welcome to *JOSEPH: A Life of Rejection, Resilience and Respect.* I am so glad you have decided to offer this study. My prayer is that you will be doubly blessed as you prepare for the women you facilitate.

Step One: Publicly promote *JOSEPH: A Life of Rejection, Resilience and Respect* four to five weeks prior to the Introduction session.

Step Two: Order workbooks and DVDs.

Step Three: Reserve meeting rooms and DVD player.

Step Four: Enlist and meet with facilitators, if needed.

Leading a Discussion Group

You do not need to be a gifted teacher or natural leader to facilitate the small-group sessions. With a warm and hospitable demeanor, you should, however, be able to help women experience God's truth and its life-changing effect by encouraging them to spend time with the Lord daily and enjoy His presence.

Before each session, view the DVD. Then prayerfully and thoroughly prepare each week's assignment before meeting with your group.

This guide will help you facilitate seven two-hour group sessions. Each DVD session will be no longer than thirty-five minutes in length and should be shown prior to the discussion time. The discussion time should be less than one hour, with the remainder of your time devoted to prayer and fellowship.

During the Introduction Session

1. As women arrive, prepare their name tags and have them pick up their copy of *JOSEPH: A Life of Rejection, Resilience and Respect.*
2. Welcome them and view the Introduction Session together. A note page is provided for taking notes during the lecture.
3. After the Introduction Session, break up into small discussion groups of ten to twelve and have the women introduce themselves to each other.
4. The facilitator should share with the women the "Four C" guidelines.
    1. **COMMITTED:** We will get so much out of this study if we come prepared for discussion, having spent time in His Word daily. May we be open to what God wants to show us in our lives (Psalm 139: 23-24).
    2. **CONSIDERATE:** We need to be considerate toward others and be willing to serve them. We should be careful about what we share so that we don't bring harm to anyone's reputation. We also don't discuss the church or denomination we belong to since there are many different churches represented. We will need to be courteous, letting others share so we will not dominate the conversation. Each of us must be sensitive to what God would have us share (Ephesians 5:21).
    3. **CONFIDENTIAL:** Let this be a place where we can feel comfortable sharing. Let's give each other the assurance that whatever we hear, we will respect their feelings. No one should worry about being the focus of criticism or gossip (Ephesians 4:29).
    4. **CHRIST-LIKE:** As we grow to know God more intimately, He will give us hope. He will change us and set us free to be all that He meant for us to be (2 Corinthians 3:18).

Suggestion: Ask these provided questions pertaining to the Introduction session.

1. What excites you about the story of Joseph?
2. What is most familiar to you about the life of Joseph?

End discussion time with prayer. Then encourage the women to prepare for next week's discussion by completing their daily assignments from Week One.

During Sessions Two - Seven

Welcome the women and view the DVD session pertaining to the week together. The note page that follows the assignment they completed during the week is provided for taking notes during the lecture.

After the DVD session, break up into small discussion groups.

You will find suggested discussion questions marked by this Coat of Many Colors symbol on each day.

These questions are formatted for the facilitator to conduct a discussion in a timely manner. You may ask additional questions as you feel led by the Holy Spirit.

End discussion time with prayer. Then encourage the women to prepare for the next week's discussion by completing their daily assignments for the next week.

During the Last Session Together

If you have a large group comprising multiple discussion groups, after viewing the DVD and before breaking up into your smaller discussion groups, you may want to have a corporate sharing time during which attendees have the opportunity to share what God has taught them through *JOSEPH: A Life of Rejection, Resilience and Respect.* This is usually an emotionally moving and encouraging time for all participants.

I would love to hear from you and the impact this study has made on you and the women you lead through *JOSEPH: A Life of Rejection, Resilience and Respect.*

- Email: jessie.seneca@gmail.com
- Facebook: More of Him Ministries
- Twitter: @JessieSeneca

INTRODUCTION

Welcome to the Bible study, *JOSEPH: A Life of Rejection, Resilience and Respect.* I am so excited that you have joined us for an in-depth look at the amazing life of Joseph. As we journey together through the last chapters of Genesis to seek out what is behind this man so many love, you will get the opportunity to apply these life lessons and motivate you to live more like Jesus.

I have a confession to make. When others found out that the Bible study I was writing is about Joseph, they told me, "Joseph's story was their favorite one in the Bible!" After hearing that comment many times, fear gripped me. Maybe, just maybe, there wasn't much more to learn. Oh my, was I wrong! Soon after researching and writing, I quickly discovered that there was so much more behind the multi-colored coat, the brothers, and the temptations. My prayer became this: that those engaged in this study would not just know the story but also be able to really apply the lessons lived out by Joseph.

The research rocked my world and cut deeper than I expected. I am now different because of my study of the life of Joseph. I am forever changed. I hope you will be also.

I primarily use the New American Standard Version of the Bible in *JOSEPH: A Life of Rejection, Resilience and Respect.* If you don't own this particular translation, you can still answer the questions without difficulty. You will find suggested discussion questions identified with a symbol like this. These are formatted for your facilitator to conduct a discussion in a timely manner.

At the end of each lesson, I encourage you to take a moment and reflect on your day's findings and consider how God wants you to respond to what He showed you that day. Through this study, God has taught me much about Himself and the continued renewal of mind, spirit, and soul that we need to seek out on a daily basis. I pray that whatever you do in word or deed, you do it all in the name of the Lord Jesus, giving thanks through Him to God the Father (Colossians 3:17).

Introductory
Video Session

Week One

Day One
A Look Back Through the Generations

Day Two
In the Ring with God

Day Three
Hold On

Day Four
Purity: A Keynote Throughout the Life of Joseph

Day Five
The Favored Son

DAY ONE

A Look Back Through the Generations

Welcome!

You may be starting this study with many preconceived ideas of the man Joseph from the Old Testament. Some of you may be thinking, "Yes, I have seen Joseph and the *Amazing Technicolor Dreamcoat,*" but you are uncertain of what characterizes the man behind the beautifully colored jacket. No matter where you may be in your knowledge of Joseph, my prayer is that all your understanding of Joseph will be heightened through this study. You will look at his life and be given the opportunity to apply his commitment, challenges, and devotion to your own life and live it out with the same resolve, resilience, and reputation of one of the most talked-about characters of the Bible.

Many years ago while I was studying Genesis, I fell in love with Joseph. I thought there must be so much more to learn if he was given fourteen chapters, over a fourth of the Bible's first book (37-50). We are going to study his life and see what gave him such determination, love for family, and desire to please God. Let's begin this journey together.

Let's start with the first mention of Joseph.

We first meet Joseph in Genesis 30:22-24. Please read it for yourself.

What important event took place in the life of Joseph?

Joseph

If we go back to the beginning of the Patriarchal Age, we can trace Joseph's lineage back through Abraham, Isaac, and Jacob, the main patriarchs of the faith. Jacob, Joseph's father, had two wives, Leah and Rachel, who were engaged in a child-bearing competition.

Read the account of the sister switch (Genesis 29:15-29).

What are the names of Laban's two daughters?

Whom did Jacob love, and what was he willing to do to gain her?

I don't want you to miss the gem hidden in Genesis 29:20. What does it say about Jacob's love for Rachel?

What deceptive act did Laban perform in Genesis 29:23?

It was customary for the bride to be adorned in veils that hid her face (except eyes) throughout the bridal week ceremony. The bride would enter her groom's chamber still adorned in veils, and under the cover of total darkness, the marriage was consummated. So in the morning, what a surprise it was for Jacob to see Leah and not Rachel.

Not only did Jacob receive two wives at the end of the bridal week, but their maids, Bilhah and Zilpah, as well, which was a customary wedding gift to a daughter. Jacob's love for Rachel outweighed his love for her sister, Leah, and so the child-bearing feud began.

Jacob sowed some bitter seeds with his coolness toward Leah, his unplanned wife. Both God and Leah were aware of the discontent of Jacob. Yet Leah was fruitful, and Rachel was barren for a season. Leah's first four sons were born in rapid succession.

Let's look at the deeper meaning behind the names of the four sons of Leah and Jacob. Read Genesis 29:32-35 and list the meaning for each son's name.

Son #1 name and meaning (v. 32)

Son #2 name and meaning (v. 33)

Son #3 name and meaning (v. 34)

Son #4 name and meaning (v. 35)

When you deeply seek the One who comforts, you can sing praises within the storm.

It is interesting to note Leah's trust in God. I believe she knew God cared for her. She recognized God as the One who gives life in spite of human efforts. And with the fourth son, she stopped wishing for her husband's attachment and approval and said, "This time I will praise the Lord." We can see the progression of Leah's personal relationship with

God as she names her sons: First, He sees her. Then He's "close" enough to hear her. Soon He is the object of her praise.

Have there been times when you've wished for another person's approval, only to come up empty-handed? Did you wish you were loved more than you are? Did you look for love outside God's protection? This is the love so many desire, but they come away feeling depleted and empty. We should desire to be more like Leah. In spite of her circumstances, she praised the Lord, and her love was found in God alone.

In a culture that considered children, especially sons, a symbol of power and prestige, jealousy loomed around every corner of Rachel's mind. So Rachel took matters into her own hands, even though she knew what happened when Jacob's grandmother, Sarah, did the same thing and Ishmael was born to her maidservant, Hagar (Genesis 16). This was like a modern-day "soap opera," right out of the pages of the Holy Bible.

For our last Scripture today, read about the surrogate mother-dilemma (Genesis 30:1-24).

What green monster reared its ugly head in verse 1 and by whom? What was her response?

How did Rachel receive her first two sons (vv. 3-8)?

Who followed in Rachel's footsteps? What did she do (vv. 9-13)?

Write in your own words what took place next (vv. 14-21).

It wasn't good enough for Leah to have four of her own sons and two from her maid- servant, totaling six. She needed more assurance, so she "one-upped" Rachel.

And so we are back to the beginning with our first question. What important event took place in Genesis 30:22-24? The birth of Joseph.

Write the meaning of Joseph's name.

But what does this line in verse 24 mean? She named him Joseph, saying, "May the Lord give me another son." The wording connects with the name of Joseph, but it almost sounds as though Rachel was praying for yet another son after Joseph. The only logical conclusion is that, unlike his brothers, Joseph was named for an event that Rachel hoped would yet occur—not for the circumstances surrounding his own birth. Some interpreters have suggested a hidden wordplay in the words taken away (v. 23), which could be a prophetic indication of Joseph's kidnapping and slavery in Egypt, but that may be more than the text can handle.[1]

To arrive at Joseph's birth on the biblical timeline, we had to look back at the steps taken by two women and the road they traveled. Some of the areas they dealt with are the same ones that we women of the twenty-first century deal with—loneliness, jealousy, deceit, lack of love, disfavor, and possibly barrenness.

Do any parts of their stories resonate with you? If yes, write a prayer back to God about what is on your heart and how you are feeling.

> *Those who look to him are radiant;*
> *their faces are never covered with shame.*
> (Psalm 34:5 NIV)

If you are dealing with any of these areas, run to the Father of all truth. Allow Him to embrace you in His loving arms and hold you tight. Find rest in a caring God.

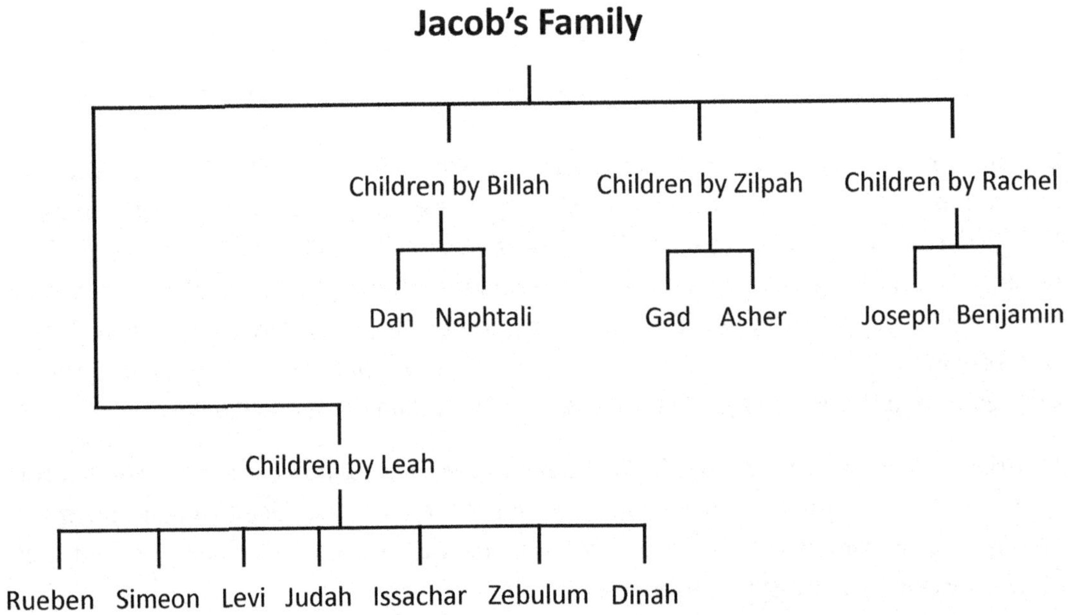

[1]Anders, Max. Holeman New Testament Commentary; Genesis. Nashville,TN: Broadman & Holeman, 2002. 250

Day Two

In the Ring with God

Joseph is considered the last in the patriarchal line, after Abraham, Isaac, and Jacob. Genesis 37-50 is the connecting link between Jacob the person and Israel the nation in Egypt.

I want us to take the next couple of days to revisit the history of Joseph's father, Jacob, whom we will study later as an old man. But today, we will see him in his prime and learn about the importance behind his name change from Jacob to Israel.

Yesterday, we read about Jacob's father-in-law, Laban, and his deceptive scheme using his two daughters, Leah and Rachel. We now see Jacob departing from Laban in Genesis 32 with his wives and children. On their way to Canaan, Jacob has an amazing encounter with the Almighty God. Then they traveled through the country of Edom, where Jacob was reunited with his twin brother, Esau, whom he deceived for the birthright (Genesis 27). Jacob's gifts and humility found favor with Esau.

Our reading for today will be Genesis 32 and 33. I know it's a little long, but it's so worth the read. Take time now to read the great embrace of two brothers and the outcome.

Retell this story in your own words.

It is always good to recap what we just read and consider how the story resonates with us. Discuss the areas from the story that spoke directly to your heart.

Jacob lived in two camps, one of fear and one of God's mighty angels. He named the place where he met with God's angels, Mahanaim (Genesis 32:2). Mahanaim means "two camps." One commentator notes that possibly the camp of fear was with the eventual meeting of his brother, Esau, on his mind, while the camp of knowing was that he was not alone or defenseless.[1]

Isn't that just like us at times—watching with one eye open and fearful of what lurks around the corner while trying to trust in God's protection?

During this season of your life, what situation are you watching fearfully and needing God's protection for?

Or,

Describe an experience in your life when you were fearful, but God opened your spiritual eyes to see that He was right by your side as you walked through the darkness that lay ahead.

According to Isaiah 45:3, what can you find in the secret place with God?

I absolutely love Isaiah 45:3 because it says that God gives us treasures and hidden wealth so that we'll realize He knows us by name. Wow! When you begin to grasp the depth of God as you meet with Him, you will be changed as you discover the power of coming to the secret place with God. It will ignite your passion and strengthen your work for Him. Please don't miss the phrase that says, treasure of darkness. Sometimes it is in the darkest hour that God reveals Himself to you in ways you never dreamed possible.

"I will give you the treasures of darkness
And hidden wealth of secret places,
So that you may know that it is I,
The Lord, the God of Israel, who calls you by your name."
(Isaiah 45:3 NASB)

So, where I want us to focus is the wrestling match between Jacob and God. In this alone moment with God, possibly a dark time in the life of Jacob, he came out shining brightly.

Re-read Genesis 32:22-32.

Whom and what did Jacob send across the Jabbok River in verses 22-23?

Sometimes we have to send everyone and everything away so we can spend quiet time with God. During these times, God needs for us to be all by ourselves so He has our full attention.

Who are you when you are alone? Are you the same person whom others view in the light of day?

I have experienced many sleepless nights when I've felt like I was having my very own wrestling match with God. There were nights I wished for the morning sunrise to appear hours before it did. And there were other nights I told God, just like Jacob did, "I will not let go until you bless me."

As we have already established, there are many treasures to be discovered while in the darkness. Some of them may not be what we want to dig up, but when they're polished up, we can come out shining with the fullness of His glory.

Share about a wrestling story with God, the outcome, and those treasures you learned about in the darkness.

We will pick back up with this wrestling match tomorrow. See you in the ring.

[1]Bible Study Fellowship: Genesis, Lesson twenty-five (San Antonio, TX: Bible Study Fellowship International, 1993). 2

Day Three

Hold On

We may have thought that the man Jacob wrestled was a mortal man at the beginning of the wrestling match, but we know better after reading Genesis 32:30. Jacob named the place where the match happened, Peniel. Peniel means I have seen God face to face, yet my life has been preserved.

Re-read Genesis 32:25-32 to reenact the match.

What did Jacob require from the man of God?

How did the man of God respond to Jacob's request?

Jacob finally surrendered in faith. God asked Jacob his name, which revealed his old character and disposition. Jacob means "deceiver" (Genesis 27:36). God wanted Jacob to see what his former name meant, but then something spectacular happened. God gave Jacob a new name—Israel, meaning "He struggled with God." Before this surrender, Jacob would prevail over people through trickery, but now he would prevail with God.

Jacob's ambition to win did not cease but changed due to an encounter with God. He had a passionate desire to hold on until the blessing came and then walk forward with power beyond himself, even if it was with a slight limp. He would walk in a new and right direction following after God, not selfish ambitions.

Do you tend to live your life thinking the thoughts of your "old self?" Do you believe what others say about you? Are they true?

When you think of the "I am" statement that best describes you, what is it? I am _____.

Is this statement true? Is it false? Have you kept it around too long?

Isn't it time you start believing what is true—what God's Word reveals about who you are?

Look up the following Scriptures and match them with the truths of God.

Isaiah 43:4	You are honored and I love you
Psalm 139:17-18	The LORD directs the steps of the godly. He delights in every detail of their lives.
Psalm 17:8	Keep me as the apple of the eye; Hide me in the shadow of Your wings
Psalm 37:23	God's thoughts about you are precious, and they outnumber the sand.
Psalm 45:11	The King is enthralled by your beauty; honor him, for he is your lord.

This is what is true! Yes, there may be some truth to your former name and ways. But God has given you a new identity and a new character when you believe in His Son, Jesus Christ. He doesn't just patch up the old, but rather He transforms us into new creations so that we can enjoy abundant life. And that is how we should be living, for in Him we live and move and have our being (Acts 17:28).

Sometimes I come out of my wrestling match with God tired and walking with a limp. But that limp has always reminded me of the battles and victories with God. For me, it is better to walk with a limp knowing that I overcame in the match, surrendered myself, and received the blessing. I can now lift my head with honor and enjoy the freedom that only God can bestow on His people.

Dear sister, if you are still in the midst of your battle, hold on tight and fight hard until the blessing comes. It will come when you surrender to His plan.

From the New Testament, please read Matthew 18:8-9. In your own words, write what Jesus said to do with a stumbling block.

Jesus was not teaching about self-mutilation. Doing that would not remove the source of offense, which is the heart. Just as Jacob had to wrestle things through with God and renounce his old name and ways, there are times when you'll have to do the same thing. Oh yes, the struggle may maim you. You may be left with a scar or limp, but if it removes the source of offense, isn't it worth it? To keep you from offending God, radical changes are often necessary. That's why you'll need to ask God to search your heart daily to see if there's anything in you that offends Him (Psalm 139:23-24).

"If your hand or your foot causes you to stumble, cut it off and throw it from you; it is better for you to enter life crippled or lame, than to have two hands or two feet and be cast into the eternal fire. If your eye causes you to stumble, pluck it out and throw it from you. It is better for you to enter life with one eye, than to have two eyes and be cast into the fiery hell."

(Matthew 18:8-9 NASB)

> *"I call heaven and earth to witness against you today, that I have set before you life and death, the blessing and the curse. So choose life in order that you may live, you and your descendants, by loving the Lord your God, by obeying His voice, and by holding fast to Him; for this is your life and the length of your days, that you may live in the land which the Lord swore to your fathers, to Abraham, Isaac, and Jacob, to give them."*
>
> (Deuteronomy 30:19-20 NASB)

According to Deuteronomy 30:19-20, what four things must we do to receive the Lord's blessing?

- **Choose** ____________________
- **Love** ____________________
- **Obey** ____________________
- ____________________ **to Him.**

The choice is up to you if you decide to choose life. Choosing life will give you the power to live for God right here and now with the view of eternity on your mind (Colossians 3:1-2). We have many blessings to reap while we have breath. To gain them, we must live life to the fullest as we love God whole-heartedly, obediently listening to His small whisper and holding onto His hand while we go around every corner.

Let's take one final look at Jacob and Rachel and the birth of their last son, Benjamin, Joseph's younger brother.

Remember Day One, when we read the meaning of Joseph's name, May the Lord give me another son (Genesis 30:24)? I bet Rachel could have hardly imagined back then that Ben-Oni would end her life.

> *Rachel was about to die, but with her last breath she named the baby Ben-oni (which means "son of my sorrow"). The baby's father, Jacob, however called him Benjamin (which means "son of my right hand").*
>
> Genesis 35:18 (NLT)

Read Genesis 35:18 and record the meaning of the names given to their last son.

Ben-Oni

Ben-jamin

In your own words, tell what you think transpired with this name change.

What Rachel thought was sorrowful, Jacob turned into triumph and victory. In addition, Jacob may have wanted to give a good name to the child who was the answer to Rachel's prayer. He may have wanted to continually look at Benjamin with good thoughts about the woman he loved so much.

As we go through this study of Joseph, both of these men, Israel (Jacob) and Benjamin, will become dear to our hearts. Tomorrow we will focus our complete attention on our main man—Joseph.

Day Four

Purity: A Keynote Throughout the Life of Joseph

We will now begin to study Joseph. This entire portion of Genesis 37-50 illustrates God's overruling of world events to fulfill His purpose in the history of Israel, which became His chosen instrument. It fulfills Jehovah's prophecy to Abraham in Genesis 15:13 (NIV), "Your descendants will be strangers in a country not their own [Egypt], and they will be enslaved and mistreated four hundred years." These events in the life of Joseph will become clear to us as we study his captivity and bondage, his elevation, and the revelation of himself to his brothers before that time when the Hebrews are led into slavery at the hands of the Egyptians for four hundred years.

Many scholars say that Joseph foreshadows the person who altogether is lovely in character, Jesus Christ. We see this through Joseph's singleness of heart, devotion to God, high morality, nobility during servitude, forgiving spirit, and modesty during promotion. In fact, his faults are hard to come by, and for this reason many say he is the prefigured epitome of Jesus. Let's begin to examine these great qualities of Joseph and see how we can apply them to our own lives.

We pick up with Joseph at the age of seventeen. Please read Genesis 37:1-4.

What was Joseph's occupation?

"Purity is not a gift—it is the result of repentance and serious pursuit of God."
~ John C. Maxwell

The first characteristic of Joseph we find in today's reading is purity. It is important to see this from the onset since it will be a keynote throughout the life of Joseph. His purity brought him much honor and blessing from God and his father, but on the other hand, it brought him much suffering from his enemies—which included his brothers.

The purity of Joseph is revealed in the validity of his report to his father regarding his brothers' evil conduct while pasturing the sheep. This particular Scripture does not share the details of their evil ways, but we can read throughout Genesis about some of the shenanigans of this evil bunch.

Read the following verses and list the brothers' evil ways.

Genesis 34:25

Genesis 35:22

Genesis 37:4

Genesis 37:11

Genesis 37:28

Genesis 37:31-33

Genesis 38:12-18

The evil hearts of these brothers (except for Benjamin, who was still young enough to be at home with his father), are revealed in their actions: murder, incest, hatred, envy, selling Joseph into slavery, lying, and immorality. Joseph must have felt morally bound and pure in heart to tell his father the evil deeds committed by his brothers while shepherding, which was not unexpected or hard to believe.

As you read this Scripture today, did it cross your mind that Joseph may have been a *tattletale*? Some accuse Joseph of tale-bearing when he came to his father with the news of his brothers. But we will see that this was not the case at all.

How do you know when something is gossip or not?

Let's answer three questions from Genesis 37:2:

Whom did Joseph speak to?

What did Joseph speak?

Why did Joseph speak?

Joseph, a faithful servant, went directly to his father. We are not told that he spoke to anyone else on his way back home. He spoke the truth, convicted and obligated to inform his father of the condition of the flock because he opposed evil.

Many times, when a certain piece of news falls under the umbrella of gossip, talebearers are always telling the wrong person. Their wrong act may not be in what they say, but to whom they say it. It does makes a difference whom you tell.

Christians can either stop evil or spread it.[1] Unfortunately, talebearers have a habit of telling evil things only to those who will spread evil, not stop it. But this is not the case with Joseph.

Gossips may involve stretching the truth, sharing with wrong motives, or telling someone something under the canopy of "prayer." We've all done it at one time or another and regretted it. In fact, you probably have said something you wanted to retract just as soon as you heard it coming out of your mouth . . . but it was too late. You couldn't even believe you uttered the words.

Read 1 Timothy 3:11 and Titus 2:3-6.

What does it say about gossiping?

Ask yourself these questions before you share something with another.

- *Whom am I speaking to?*
- *What am I speaking?*
- *Why am I speaking?*

Just as Joseph was honest and upright in his sharing, so should we. If we are apt to share something and doesn't feel right, we should ask ourselves these three little questions: Whom am I speaking to? What am I speaking? Why am I speaking? These three questions can keep you out of unnecessary troubles.[2]

As much as I want to call it a day, feeling the heaviness of conviction, there is hope through forgiveness (1 John 1:9).

Let's make one more point about the character of Joseph. Near the end of Jacob's life, as Jacob blessed his sons, he said that Joseph was "separate from his brothers" (49:26 ESV).

Yes, he was! Most notably, he was separate from them in his conduct, which we will continue to explore in the days ahead. But for now Joseph stood alone. He refused to go along with the crowd (his brothers). In fact, no one had experienced more peer pressure than Joseph did. In the same way, let the Word of God be the standard by which you determine your conduct and actions, not peer pressure.

Women must likewise be dignified, not malicious gossips, but temperate, faithful in all things.

(1 Timothy 3:11 NASB)

May you and I dare to be pure in heart and actions as Joseph was, even when it's not the popular thing to do, but the right thing. We should dare to live as the Word says, not as the world dictates. Don't you all desire to be women of strong character, living lives of purity?

Older women likewise are to be reverent in their behavior, not malicious gossips nor enslaved to much wine, teaching what is good, so that they may encourage the young women to love their husbands, to love their children, to be sensible, pure, workers at home, kind, being subject to their own husbands, so that the word of God will not be dishonored.

(Titus 2:3-5 NASB)

Finish out the day by reading 1 Timothy 4:11-12.

"Prescribe and teach these things. Let no one look down on your youthfulness, but rather in speech, conduct, love, faith and purity, show yourself an example of those who believe."

What example does God require you to live?

How will you live it out?

Now go be that example to a watching world.

[1]John G. Butler, Joseph: The Patriarch of Character (Clinton, Iowa: Regular Baptist Press, 1993), 16.

[2]Ibid, 16.

Day Five

The Favored Son

I have a beautiful jacket a family friend blessed me with one day. To my surprise, after driving near our destination, we had pulled up to a fur shop. I was then told to choose a coat of my liking. After receiving this beautiful coat, I wore it with such honor and took impeccable care of it. I should wear it more than I do, but I only seem to wear it on special occasions. Probably just like Joseph, when wearing this special jacket, I feel a bond with those who gave it to me.

We now come to the section of Genesis that may be the most well-known part of Joseph's story—his richly ornamented coat, his multi-colored tunic that is better known as the coat of many colors. I don't know that we will get much past Genesis 37:3 and 4 today, but we will learn much about the significance of the coat, the qualifications for the coat, and the gospel significance in the coat.

Read Genesis 37:3-4.

List all that you know about the beautiful coat given to Joseph from his father, Jacob.

The coat given to Joseph distinguishes him as the favorite son. Jacob favored Joseph because he was the son of his old age by his beloved wife, Rachel. Also, Joseph had character, which we saw yesterday, that his brothers did not have.

Jacob made no qualms about presenting Joseph with the beautiful coat. From my reading, most scholars agree that the tunic was a long-sleeved coat with elegant embroidered trim that reached down to the ankles. The coat represented several different things:

- **It signified rank.** Your common person would most likely wear something shorter and sleeveless, which would make their work easier to perform. By giving Joseph this jacket, Jacob was implying, "You can wear this beautiful garment and not work as hard as your brothers."[1]
- **It symbolizes leadership.** Joseph was respected because of his spiritual qualifications and convictions, unlike Reuben, who should have received it as the eldest son. However, due to an act of incest which disqualified him in Genesis 35:22, he was not in line for it anymore. There could only be one ornamented robe per family, and Joseph wore it with confidence.
- **The gospel in the coat.**[2]

Read Isaiah 61:10 (NASB) and write the similarities between Joseph's robe and the robe the believer is given.

I will rejoice greatly in the Lord,
My soul will exult in my God;
For He has clothed me with garments of salvation,
He has wrapped me with a robe of righteousness,
As a bridegroom decks himself with a garland,
And as a bride adorns herself with her jewels.

Isaiah 61:10 (NASB)

Read what John Butler writes about this beautiful coat:

> No coat is so beautiful; for it is a robe of righteousness and therefore, has the "beauty of holiness" (Psalm 29:2). This robe, like Joseph's, exempts the believer from labor but not from service (see Matthew 11:28-30). And as Joseph's robe speaks of rank, so does this robe; for we are a "royal priesthood" (1 Peter 2:9), and we shall rule and reign with Christ in the millennium (Revelation 20:6). The robe of righteousness attires us appropriately for the position we gain through Jesus Christ in our salvation.[3]

All of this is such a blessing upon Joseph, but it came at the expense of his brothers. Put yourself in their shoes as you watch all this unfold over the last seventeen years: A father's love is showered on one out of twelve sons. A father's care is given to what could be considered the "middle child," but instead he is elevated to the level of the eldest and respected son.

I'm not saying that it wasn't deserved. But Jacob could have been a little more discreet, don't you think?

Read the following Scriptures and write down what they say about partiality and favoritism.

Deuteronomy 10:16-18

Acts 10:34-35

James 2:1-3, 9

You may be reading this and think to yourself, This is the story that I have lived—parental favoritism. A father's oversight, intentional or not, still hurts and cuts to the bone. So does a mother's "busyness" that keeps her from attending to your needs. But thankfully our heavenly Father is a God who's impartial to race, age, rank, or beauty. You can rest in that truth!

Jacob's actions, taken this early in Joseph's life, would seem to be unwise. Jacob should have remembered what parental favoritism does to a family. It separated him from his

My brethren, do not hold your faith in our glorious Lord Jesus Christ with an attitude of personal favoritism. For if a man comes into your assembly with a gold ring and dressed in fine clothes, and there also comes in a poor man in dirty clothes, and you pay special attention to the one who is wearing the fine clothes, and say, "You sit here in a good place," and you say to the poor man, "You stand over there, or sit down by my footstool"...

(James 2:1-3 NASB)

> *Our heavenly Father is a God who's impartial to race, age, rank, or beauty. You can rest in that truth!*

loving mother, Rebekah (Genesis 27:1-28:5), and it would, in time, separate Joseph from Jacob.

We will close today by looking at Joseph's brothers.

Re-read Genesis 37:4 and explain the progression of their attitude.

Because of their father's actions, the jealousy of Joseph's half-brothers turned to resentment and hatred, to the extent that they could not even speak a kind word to him. They despised him so much that they could not even make a friendly gesture. Imagine the building pressure in their home. The explosive internal device was ready to erupt, and erupt it would.

Unless it's recognized and dealt with, jealousy will cause us to act in ways we never thought we would.

Read James 3:13-17 and describe what happens as a result of jealousy.

What is the opposite of jealousy? What should it look like in a believer's life?

We all deal with hurts, and if not handled properly, our hurts will turn into resentment and jealousy. Oh, that you would seek your heavenly Father for the healing of your emotional pain, wound, or devastation and let Him reach down and touch those injured parts of your spirit you never knew existed. By allowing Him access into your daily life and thoughts, you will be able to face those who have rejected you, those you feel threatened by, or maybe those you've even been bullied by. You will be able to walk in a manner worthy of your calling. Do yourself a favor. Forgive! It really doesn't matter whose fault it is anyway.

Who among you is wise and understanding? Let him show by his good behavior his deeds in the gentleness of wisdom. But if you have bitter jealousy and selfish ambition in your heart, do not be arrogant and so lie against the truth. This wisdom is not that which comes down from above, but is earthly, natural, demonic. For where jealousy and selfish ambition exist, there is disorder and every evil thing. But the wisdom from above is first pure, then peaceable, gentle, reasonable, full of mercy and good fruits, unwavering, without hypocrisy.

(James 3:13-17 NASB)

---

[1]John G. Butler, Joseph: The Patriarch of Character (Clinton, Iowa: Regular Baptist Press, 1993), 19, 20.

[2]Ibid., 19, 20.

[3]Ibid., 21, 22.

WEEK ONE
VIDEO SESSION

PRINCIPLE 1:

WHEN FEELING **REJECTED**, REMEMBER,
HE HAS LAID HIS HAND UPON YOU.

Week TWO

Day One
Dream Giver

Day Two
The Valor of Pursuit

Day Three
It All Begins in the Heart

Day Four
Look Up When Down

Day Five
A Leader Is Trained Through Suffering

Day One

Dream Giver

Have you ever had a dream placed in your heart by God? Or perhaps God has revealed something to you through a dream or vision. These are two very different things. You may feel God calling you to do something, and He places it on your heart so that you'll work diligently toward the goal. Yet that is different than God speaking to you in a dream.

What happens to Joseph in today's reading is the latter of the two. Several generations prior to Joseph, his great-great-grandfather, Abraham, also had a dream (15:13) regarding his nation being placed under Egyptian bondage. Then his father Jacob had a dream that God would protect and prosper him as he sojourned with Laban (28:12, 15).

In Old Testament times, God spoke more through dreams because they did not have the written Word of God, the divine revelation from the heavenly Father, which we have today. This is not to say that God can't and won't reveal Himself to someone today through a dream, but we need to be careful not to allow ourselves to become so all about the "dream" that we forget the Dream Giver. God has given us the most colorful, detailed, and trustworthy possession in His divinely inspired Word—the Bible. So let us become more excited about the written Word rather than searching for the interpretation of a specific dream. He will reveal Himself to us individually as we seek Him (John 14:21).

Read Hebrews 1:1-4. In these last days (between the first and second coming of Christ), how does God speak?

Read Genesis 37:5-11 to become familiar with the dreams given to Joseph.

List the responses by the following people:

Joseph

Joseph's brothers

Jacob

He who has My commandments and keeps them is the one who loves Me; and he who loves Me will be loved by My Father, and I will love him and will disclose Myself to him."

(John 14:21 NASB)

As if his brothers didn't already despise him enough, Joseph just added salt to their wounds by sharing his dreams with them and their father and mother. Joseph's brothers hated him that much more. In fact, verses 5-10 mentioned three times that Joseph's brothers hated him and became jealous of him. Now, since they were already on unfriendly terms with Joseph (v. 4), don't you think Joseph should have been a little more careful and discerning about what he shared and how he shared it?

Has God ever placed something on your heart that you shared with others prematurely? What was the outcome?

Why do you think God may not want us to share the details of every vision He has placed within us?

At some point in our lives, we all have shared information too early. The timing was not right and/or perhaps others weren't ready to hear it. It's a hard lesson to learn. Yet through the story we are unfolding today, this could be the very lesson we can take away: We should learn to discern what to reveal and what to retain concerning His personal revelation to us. We need to be sensitive to what God wants to keep between us and Him and what He wants us to share. When the time is right, it will be all about the delivery of the message. Will it be shared with a spirit of humility, or arrogance?

> *We should learn to discern what to reveal and what to retain concerning His personal revelation to us.*

Read Matthew 7:6 and explain in your own words what this verse is saying to you.

The various commentaries about Joseph subscribe to one of two views pertaining to this passage of Scripture about his revealed dreams. Either they say that Joseph is a young, innocent seventeen-year old boy who's unaware of his effects on those around him, or he is an arrogant, spoiled brat rudely flaunting his status in the family.

> *Do not give what is holy to dogs, and do not throw your pearls before swine, or they will trample them under their feet, and turn and tear you to pieces.*
>
> (Matthew 7:6 NASB)

What do you think about Joseph in Genesis 37:5-11? Is he pure or proud? Explain your position.

You will be hard-pressed to find anything negative written in the Bible about Joseph. In fact, the flaws of Joseph—as well as Ruth, Esther, and Daniel—are never directly mentioned. So, I tend to take the view of a pure and righteous Joseph. No matter what you or I may think, however, the brothers did not receive it well, did they?

What do these Scriptures say regarding the pure in heart?

Matthew 5:8

Psalm 24:3-5

Proverbs 21:7-9

What are some adjectives that come to your mind when you think of the word "pure"?

Do you think that words and phrases such as wholesome, untainted by immorality, and free of any contamination are fitting for Joseph? Are they fitting for you? When we read that God's Word is purified seven times (Psalm 12:6), how can we not want to live by every word written? His statutes and commands are meant for our good and to help us stay pure. He does not want us "to be conformed to this world, but to be transformed by the renewing of our mind, so that we can prove what the will of God is, that which is good and acceptable and perfect" (Romans 12:2).

Re-read Genesis 37:6-11 and write in your own words the meaning of the dreams.

Dream #1

Dream #2

This is what Erwin W. Lutzer writes about the two dreams:

> The scene of the first dream was agricultural, perhaps a hint of the manner in which Joseph's authority over his brothers would be achieved. The second dream was celestial: the sun, moon and stars bowed down to him. His father, his mother, his brothers, yes, they would all bow down to him. He would be above the whole house of Jacob.[1]

As we will see in the weeks to come, these dreams were fulfilled but not without much hardship. God was so good to give Joseph both dreams, with the second confirming the first, as well as the divine repetition to assure Joseph of the facts, which would carry him through the next thirteen years—in and out of persecution.

[1]Erwin W. Lutzer, Keep Your Dream Alive: Lessons from the Life of Joseph (Grand Rapids, MI: Kregel Publications, 2003) 27, 28.

Day Two

The Valor of Pursuit

Before moving on from our study of the effects Joseph's dreams had on his family, let's just hit one more area.

Even though there was a split in the family, God used these dreams—yes, even despite the unwise actions of Joseph—to accomplish His purpose. God is never taken by surprise by our foolish decisions. God's purpose for Joseph's life would be accomplished regardless of Joseph's approach.

But even still, Joseph must have felt some sadness because of his brothers' hatred and his father's rebuke. Jacob and Joseph had always been so amicable toward each other. Yet this sudden rift between the two involved opposition from an unexpected source that was hard to swallow, and that always cuts a little deeper. Joseph may have thought that his father would have received the dream better than he did and embrace his son's revelation, but despite the rejection, you will still find Joseph honoring his father.

Have you ever been hurt by a family member, close friend, co-worker, or ministry partner? If so, how did you handle it?

Read Psalm 55:12-23. How did David deal with the hurt caused by a close companion? How is God asking you to apply this to your life?

Moving on . . .

Read Genesis 37:12-36 to become familiar with this week's reading. Recap this story in your own words. (*We will take the next few days to break this down.*)

The last we heard of Joseph's brothers was that they were jealous of him (v. 11). Now we see the brothers trekking back fifty miles from Hebron to Shechem to pasture their animals on a small piece of property that still belongs to their family. I am sure a well-deserved break from each other was needed at this time. Shechem was the very place where their sister, Dinah, had been defiled and raped, which resulted in Simeon and Levi taking matters into their own hands and killing all the men, as well as raiding their goods (Genesis 34).

After Jacob realized where they had gone, he may have thought that they were in great danger because of the vengeful action they had taken against the men of Shechem. Even though Jacob was well aware of the hatred his sons harbored against Joseph, he still sent Joseph off to see about his brothers' welfare. Didn't Jacob have any idea of the danger he was sending Joseph, his favorite son, into? Actually, one could say that Jacob set Joseph up for what was about to happen to him.

What was Joseph's response to his father (v. 13)?

Do you think your response would have been as noble?

Traveling to Shechem to check on his brothers, as his father asked, required considerable character on Joseph's part.

Circle the character qualities that stand out in Joseph through his one little statement: "*I will go.*"

Submission Humility Sacrifice Steadfastness Selfishness Faithfulness

Not only did Joseph go to Shechem in a valorous pursuit, but then he went on to Dothan, another fifteen miles farther from Hebron. Joseph's response, "I will go" showed his humility and proved that the possession of the multi-colored coat did not go to his head and puff him up with pride. Joseph was willing to submit to his father's request, and then he stayed true to the task.

What does Exodus 33:15 say about going?

Do you think Joseph thought this before he left for Shechem? Have you ever thought this as you went into unknown territory? I have been presented many times with a task I was unsure about or knew I couldn't do in my own strength. Because I needed God to go before me, I even went one step further, asking Him to be there waiting for me.

Share about a time you wouldn't go unless God's presence went with you.

From the following Scriptures what do you learn about the qualities Joseph must have possessed? Is there an area in which you lack? If so, what do you need to do to develop it?

Proverbs 15:33

Romans 12:1-2

1 Corinthians 4:2

Just as Joseph exemplified these qualities, we should desire to live them out in our own lives.

There were many things that struck me in my research, but this one area in particular. I seemed to miss each time I've read this story, and I want to share it with you.

One commentator pointed out that Joseph needed courage to go where he was asked and to wear what he wore. First of all, he went to a place where the hatred of his brothers was intense. Second, he wore his coat out of respect for his position in the family—not because of pride, but propriety. Due to the source of hostility he was about to encounter, it would take much courage to wear the coat, but Joseph wore it anyway.[1]

For me, the much-needed lesson involves appropriate dress for Christians today.

Again from *Joseph: The Patriarch of Character*, John W. Butler writes,

> Christians ought to dress like Christians and look like Christians. The popularity of immodest, sloppy, slovenly, and unkempt dress styles amongst Christians says many present-day saints are not doing well here. Joseph's brothers recognized him even

> though he was some distance away (v. 18), doubtless because of his coat. Unlike Joseph, many professing saints cannot be recognized even when they are right next to them because their appearance is so worldly. It takes courage to dress *(and act)* as a Christian should. Decent attire may bring sneers from the world, but the Christian's duty is to dress properly anyway. Joseph did *(emphasis mine)*.[2]

Dear sister, it is not just our external dress that distinguishes us as Christians but also our spiritual attire. Do others notice you from a distance and even more so when you are in the same room? Do you have the boldness of Joseph to go to places outside your comfort zone, knowing that the Lord will go with you (Joshua 1:5)?

Read 1 Peter 3:2-4 and Colossians 3:12-14. List the characteristics in these verses for which you want to be known.

Oh, that we would be clothed in light through our actions and deeds to a watching world!

> On the other hand, I am writing a new commandment to you, which is true in Him and in you, because the darkness is passing away and the true Light is already shining. The one who says he is in the Light and yet hates his brother is in the darkness until now. The one who loves his brother abides in the Light and there is no cause for stumbling in him.
>
> (1 John 2:8-10)

. . . as they observe your chaste and respectful behavior. Your adornment must not be merely external—braiding the hair, and wearing gold jewelry, or putting on dresses; but let it be the hidden person of the heart, with the imperishable quality of a gentle and quiet spirit, which is precious in the sight of God.

(1 Peter 3:2-4 NASB)

[1]John G. Butler, Joseph: The Patriarch of Character (Clinton, Iowa: Regular Baptist Press, 1993), 29.
[2]Ibid.

Day Three

It All Begins in the Heart

Have you ever been in a situation in which your thoughts became your actions? Of course you have! You have probably wished that some of those situations could be reversed. Today, we will explore the thought process of Joseph's brothers as they viewed their brother from a distance and sarcastically referred to him as the dreamer (37:19).

From our previous readings of Genesis 37, we know that the brothers' destructive thought process began earlier than that moment when they saw Joseph approaching them in Dothan. It really started once hatred and jealousy entered their hearts. The difficult part for Joseph was that he had no control over being the firstborn to Rachel, the beloved wife of Jacob, or his father's favoritism that was evidenced by the coat. He never jockeyed for position in the family but was freely given it by his father. Joseph was granted many valuable privileges, but along with those privileges came persecution.

Re-read Genesis 37:18-30 and answer the following questions.

What was the brother's original plot against Joseph?

Who were the two brothers who saved Joseph from immediate death by the hands of the others?

Describe the emotions the brothers experienced toward Joseph when they threw him into the pit. (See also Genesis 42:21-22.)

Do you think the distance from their hometown in Hebron made it easier for the brothers to go through with their plan? Why?

We will continue with the questions, but I want to take a short break to think about those we have answered thus far.

Because they were far from home, the brothers could do with Joseph as they pleased, right? Jacob was not there to stop them from taking this action. Who would know? This is the same rationale some people use today. Once they get away from home, their conduct worsens.

I have heard about this kind of rationalization from countless parents who send their eighteen-year-olds off to college. They don't know what their children are doing on a daily basis, but some of the reports are unfavorable.

However, it's not just our students who think this way but many of us at some point. Sometimes we believe that when we're away from the restrictions of home, anything goes. But what all of us need to remember is that we are never far enough away from the eye of the Almighty. He sees all, knows all, and will judge all.

"Am I a God who is near,"
declares the Lord,
"And not a God far off?
"Can a man hide himself in
hiding places
So I do not see him?" declares
the Lord.
"Do I not fill the heavens and the
earth?" declares the Lord.
(Jeremiah 23:23-24 NASB)

Read Psalm 139:7-12 and Jeremiah 23:23-24 to support this message and write it out in your own words.

Back to our questions from Genesis 37:18-30.

Explain the thinking process of the brothers that led to their actions.

The evil thoughts (hatred and jealousy) that began in the brothers' hearts corrupted them. This holds true for us as well. If our thoughts go unchecked, they will dictate our emotions and produce ill actions. In other words, evil thoughts must be stopped, or they will lead to evil conduct. We must take control of our thoughts in life if we want to season our conversation with goodness and produce worthy conduct.

We must take control of our thought life if we want to season our conversation with goodness and produce worthy conduct.

Thoughts (good or bad) → Words → Conduct

Look up Ephesians 4:22-24 and James 1:14-15. How do these Scriptures instruct us to break the chain of bad conduct?

I just loved this excerpt from Erwin W. Lutzer. I could not say it any better.

> Most often hatred is fueled by the inner torments of the soul, the insecurities and anger that come from an unwillingness to yield to the will of God. The seeds of hatred lie buried in every human heart, and grow when watered with envy, jealousy, and self-will. Hatred doesn't need a reason; it feeds on itself within a selfish heart. Sometimes a person who hates is simply reflecting his own twisted emotions.[1]

So, we read that the thoughts of the brothers turned into words. They said to one another, "Here comes this dreamer! Now then let us kill him and throw him into one of the pits; and we will say, 'A wild beast devoured him.' Then let us see what will become of his dreams!" (37:19-20).

The brothers lived out the formula: thoughts → words → conduct. This is pure MEANNESS of the heart on the brothers' end.

Reuben, the eldest son of Jacob, was one of the two brothers who saved Joseph from death—all because of a change of heart. But where did he go from there? Why didn't he follow through? Was it because he lacked commitment? Reuben would keep Joseph alive, but he was still trapped in a pit of despair with the end result being his looming death.

What more could Reuben have done?

Later on, in Genesis 42:21-22, we read Reuben's words once again. What did he say to his brothers?

This is just another sign pointing to the bad character on the brothers' part and their lack of immediate obedience. If only Reuben would have followed through on his intentions, things could have been different.

Ouch! I know this day has allowed for some real self-reflection on my part. How about you?

Write a prayer of genuine confession for any area in which God is speaking to you today.

Return, O Israel, to the Lord your God,
For you have stumbled because of your iniquity.
Take words with you and return to the Lord.
Say to Him, Take away all iniquity
And receive us graciously,
That we may present the fruit of our lips.

(Hosea 14:1-2)

Thankfully, our God is a gracious God, ready to receive our confessions and provide forgiveness, which is high on His character list (1 John 1:9).

[1]Erwin W. Lutzer, Keep Your Dream Alive: Lessons from the Life of Joseph (Grand Rapids, MI: Kregel Publications, 2003), 34.

Day Four

Look Up When Down

After the brothers lowered Joseph into the pit, they sat down and ate a meal together. Their hatred for Joseph overpowered their conscience but not their appetites. I wonder if they sat there, hearing the distress of Joseph, and just were too numb to feel any empathy toward him.

We still have lessons to learn from yesterday's Scripture (37:18-30).

Re-read Genesis 37:25-30 and answer the following questions.

Which brother took over in the absence of Reuben?

What was his grandiose idea?

Why kill Joseph when they could sell him and make an immediate profit? So they sold him for twenty pieces of silver, which was the price you would pay for a handicapped slave in those days.[1] They turned him over to a group of strangers, Midianite traders, with no regrets.

Besides the jealousy the brothers had for Joseph, what else do you think could have been the reason behind the actions of the brothers? (There is not a right or wrong answer, only your opinion.)

Look up the following Scriptures and discuss the contrast within the verses.

Ezekiel 33:18-19

1 John 1:5

When the righteous turns from his righteousness and commits iniquity, then he shall die in it. But when the wicked turns from his wickedness and practices justice and righteousness, he will live by them.

(Ezekiel 33:18-19 NASB)

Selling Joseph into slavery was the brothers' way of trying to expel righteousness. Wrongdoing does not like to have righteousness nearby. By disposing him through the Midianites, they probably felt that his blood would not be on their own hands and Joseph's dreams would be dead. I just can't imagine how Joseph's brothers kept these secrets for nearly twenty years.

Even though the brothers meant their treacherous act for harm, we will see that God meant it for good. Instead of dying, Joseph was preserved alive!

We leave this scene with Joseph being abandoned by his brothers and left at the mercy of thoughtless mercenaries, who took him to a foreign land where he did not know the language and culture.

What do you think Joseph's thoughts were as he rode away with the foreign caravan?

I know what my thoughts would have been—ones of despair, doubt, self-pity, and "woe is me." But what we have learned about Joseph thus far (even though sadness captured his mind) was that he most likely still believed in the dreams God had given him. Although unsure how it would all unfold, he was still trusting God to deliver on His promise.

From the following Scriptures, tell what we are supposed to do during times of despair.

Psalm 25:15

Psalm 50:15

As I have read and re-read this story, I've thought about the message Joseph would have sent his aging father, whom he may never have gotten the chance to see again. What do you think he would have written him?

Joseph has only begun to experience the "dark events" of his life. But through all of them, you and I will see the hand of God upon his life and be able to trace His sovereign plan.

Take a moment and discuss how you have seen the hand of God on your own life.

As you look back over your life, have there been times when you've seen the mighty hand of God, but in the middle of it all, you had no clue how it would work out? It may not have been what you hoped for, but God knew what was best. He knew what would draw you closer to Him and what would make you more like His child.

Looking back, I am so glad God didn't unfold my entire life before me. Yet He gave me just enough grace and light for the moment I needed it.

Close out today by pondering on the following Scriptures. Share what each one means to you.

Joshua 4:24

Psalm 139:4-5

Psalm 143:5-6

See you tomorrow, back on the pages of Genesis as we look at Jacob's response to the evil deeds of his sons.

I remember the days of old;
I meditate on all that you have done;
I ponder the work of your hands.
I stretch out my hands to you;
my soul thirsts for you like a parched land. Selah
(Psalm 143:5-6 ESV)

[1]Charles R. Swindoll, Joseph: The Man of Integrity and Forgiveness (Nashville: Thomas Nelson, 1998), 15.

Day Five

A Leader Is Trained through Suffering

"It is doubtful that God can greatly use a man until He has greatly hurt him."
—A. W. Tozer

Even though Joseph's earthly father was not with him, his Heavenly Father crossed over the border into Egypt with Joseph and would remain with him for the next twenty years, in and out of persecution.

Read Genesis 37:29-36 and let's finish out this chapter. List the response of each of these persons to the sale of Joseph to the Midianites.

Reuben

The other brothers

Jacob

Sons and daughters

Joseph

We clearly see how one sin was linked to the next one, and then the next, and so on. (Indeed, sin comes in clusters.) From the onset of hatred and envy entering the brothers' hearts, deception followed close behind, and even murder was then contemplated by the brothers. After that, they engaged in ongoing deceit. In the case of Joseph, the brothers could lie to their father, but again we see they cannot lie to the Lord.

Sin that is concealed—in this case, for twenty years—will fester, spread, and defile.

Look up James 1:14-15 and explain the progression of temptation.

Have you ever allowed a secret sin to manifest itself, if so, what toll did it take on you and others?

I know what you are thinking. That was a hard and very personal question. Ladies, you have no idea how difficult it was for me to even write that question with those conflicting emotions flooding my soul. At any rate, even if you haven't concealed your own secret, you most likely have kept another's. But it takes its toll on you. You can't share their sin with others, so you can only encourage those people by pointing them in the right direction and speaking truth into their lives.

The effects of the brothers' evil actions caused so much heartache and suffering for many:

Joseph suffered. He endured many years of separation from his family, as well as persecution by the hands of evil men. But God's hand was always upon him, and he would rise above it all to become one of the greatest leaders ever known.

Joseph's father suffered. Verses 34 and 35 say, So Jacob tore his clothes, and put sackcloth on his loins and mourned for his son many days. And Jacob said, "Surely

I will go down to Sheol in mourning for my son." So his father wept for him. Jacob carried heavy sorrow for the loss of Joseph throughout the next twenty-plus years.

Joseph's brothers suffered. They suffered years of agonizing guilt, carrying a burden too heavy for them to bear. This suffering may not have been mentioned on the printed pages of the Old Testament, but we see it expressed by their response in Genesis 42:21: Then they said to one another, "Truly we are guilty concerning our brother, because we saw the distress of his soul when he pleaded with us, yet we would not listen; therefore this distress has come upon us." Guilt is indeed a cruel oppressor that takes the pleasure out of everyday life.

If you are dealing with some sort of guilt, there is hope for you. Be honest before God and with those who may have been affected by your sinful acts. Previously, we established that freedom is a result of being honest. God already knows; He just wants you to be honest before Him.

Look up the following Scriptures and record their truths.

Micah 7:8

Psalm 32:5

Freedom is a result of being honest.

Yes, it is hard to deal with our "stuff." Oh, but how grateful we are that there is an outlet. Romans 7:24-25 (NIV) gives us great comfort: What a wretched man I am! Who will rescue me from this body that is subject to death? Thanks be to God, who delivers me through Jesus Christ our Lord! The answer is Jesus, and we can stand on that truth!

> *"But the seed in the good soil, these are the ones who have heard the word in an* honest *and good heart, and hold it fast, and bear fruit with perseverance"*
>
> *(Luke 8:15 emphasis mine).*

One last lesson from today's portion of reading:

No one can kill a dream that God has given to you! Joseph was given a dream by God that was unstoppable. Sometimes others' hateful efforts can cause us to despair. But God will even cause dreams to surface out of misunderstandings and rejection. They may not be the dreams we choose, but they are God's dreams, nonetheless. If He is the source of the dreams, they are secure.

Which dreams/desires in your life still haven't come to fruition?

What are you doing in that time you're waiting for them to materialize?

> *God's dreams are up to God to fulfill. Step out of His way and let Him have His say.*

Ladies, God's dreams are up to Him to fulfill. Step out of His way and let Him have His say. Continue to seek Him, pray, and read His Word. Then watch Him do His work. When He feels you are ready, He will open the door so wide, you'll know without a shadow of a doubt that it is meant for you.

Press on, dear sisters!

Week Two
Video Session

Principle 2:

"When **Resolve** comes from a deep dedication in your heart toward God, He will protect you and open the way when there seems to be no way."

Week Three

Day One

Triumph Over Adversity

Day Two

Eye Candy: Sweet or Sour?

Day Three

You Can Be Triumphant Over Temptation

Day Four

Keeping in the Presence of God

Day Five

Circumstances Shouldn't Imprison Our Hearts

Day One

Triumph Over Adversity

I'm sure you're glad we're moving on from Genesis 37, even though we've gained a much better understanding of the traumatizing effects of favoritism, the nurturing of jealousy and its terrible pitfalls, the unwise decision to cover sin with more sin, and God's prevailing plan. As we go into chapter 39, we will continue to see God's mighty hand upon Joseph and his steadfast character of resolve, resilience, and respect. There is so much more to learn from Joseph's story that we can apply to our own personal lives.

We are not going to take the time to study Genesis 38, even though it is an important part of Israel's history. I would encourage you to read chapter 38 on your own time, though, for a most intriguing story about Judah (Joseph's brother) and Tamar. In Genesis 39-41 the ongoing tale of Joseph unfolds while the shocking events of chapter 38 are occurring.

> ***Read Genesis 39:1-6a. What repeated phrase indicates that the hand of God was upon Joseph and those who were blessed by Him? Support your answer using the verses.***

We now meet Joseph after he is bought by Potiphar, captain of Pharaoh's bodyguard. We don't know how long Joseph has lived in this prestigious home, but it was certainly long enough for him to rise to the top because of his sterling character. It was obvious that Joseph knew if he served Potiphar well, he was serving God well. He served with such integrity and faithfulness, despite what his brothers meant for harm, that he was promoted as Potiphar's personal assistant. Also, the blessing upon Joseph even overflowed onto the household he kept. He not only adjusted to his new surroundings, but he flourished in it.

Why do you think Joseph flourished in a difficult situation?

Let's face it; life for Joseph was not easy. Yet we never once read of him complaining. Clearly, God was the secret of Joseph's success. Even though Joseph didn't have the written Word of God to read daily, he had His presence and the dreams to hold onto. If a man of Joseph's caliber had to undergo character training through lowliness and difficulty, then we should expect to receive the same kind of training in our own lives today. In other words, we should not allow a lowly position to keep us from persevering with our dream, even when we're so discouraged that we want to give up and quit. Through the wonderful example of Joseph, we are encouraged to keep keeping on, even when circumstances are not always on our side.

Read Joshua 1:8-9 and explain what true success is in the sight of God.

There was a time in my walk with God some years back when it was hard for me to see the benefits of unnecessary persecution and unjust suffering. I felt that I didn't deserve the hurtful accusations thrown at me. I had done all that I was asked to do with much devotion and passion. I was broken down and distressed to the point of wondering, Could God ever use me again?

Yes, I felt beaten down.

But thankfully, there were strong individuals who encouraged me and guided me in the right direction. The one thing I kept saying to myself throughout the time of difficulty was, I want to be the best learner I can be.

Today, as I look back over that time and all that God has taught me since then, I know that He was training me for this time right now. Just as God was carefully training Joseph for future service, He was training me for greater things to come. He was training me to triumph over adversity.

That situation taught me how to treat my fellow leaders with gratitude and respect. As many books I have read on leadership, nothing prepared me for ministry better than the bumps and bruises I learned along the way. Just maybe what others meant for harm really benefited me for good. It's not always an easy ride, but if we continue to look up to God and allow Him to fill our thoughts and illuminate our path, He will make the way clearer. How we respond to unfairness reveals our closeness to God.

How we respond to unfairness reveals our closeness to God.

Share about a time when you felt that you suffered unjustly and discuss what you learned from it. (This may be an encouragement to someone in your group.)

Oh, that we would have faith in God that He would change our attitude to focus on triumph instead of tragedy. Let's choose to experience a new victory and new understanding of faith as we trust God with the outcome through the circumstances.

Read 2 Corinthians 1:8-11.

What was Paul's secret to surviving?

This secret is the same for you and me: God will deliver you. In the Greek, "deliver" (rhoumai) means "to draw to oneself."[1] He will draw you unto Himself and strengthen you as you rely on Him and not yourself.

And that is exactly what God did for Joseph. Whether it was Potiphar's house or prison, God prospered Joseph.

Let's close our lesson by looking at the ways the hand of God works in our lives. We are just scratching the surface regarding God's hand upon Joseph, and we will certainly see it throughout his life. But what about your own life?

Are there times when you wonder, God, where are You? What are You up to? Do You even care? If you are honest with yourself and God, you probably have answered yes to one or all of those questions.

Now, let's break down Psalm 139 into individual sections and give them a closer look.

Read Psalm 139 in its entirety.

List all the ways you see the *Omniscience* (all-knowing) attribute of God from Psalm 139:1-6.

List all the ways you see the *Omnipresence* (presence everywhere) attribute of God from Psalm 139:7-12.

List all the ways you see the *Omnipotence* (unlimited power) attribute of God from Psalm 139:13-18.

List all the ways you see the *Holiness* attribute of God from Psalm 139:19-24.

Yes, ladies, you have just come face to face with a very personal God who knows every move you make. He knows your whole day's activities. He knows the words you will utter. Indeed, the hand of God goes from confining (v. 5) to guiding (v. 10). He knit you together, so He is a vital part of the everyday details of your life. He wants what's best for you, or He would not have said that His precious thoughts of you outnumber the sand (v. 18).

Stay close to Him, enjoy His presence and trust Him with the particulars.

Allow this intimate God to search you and know your heart. He already knows your anxiety level hits the roof on some days. Be honest before Him and allow Him to lead you. Stay close to Him, enjoy His presence, and trust Him with the particulars.

[1]The New Strong's Exhaustive Concordance of the Bible.

Day Two

Eye Candy: Sweet or Sour?

Joseph's wise reaction to his situation was to maintain his good work habits. He could have wallowed in his own self-pity as he went from being a prince to a pauper, but he didn't. The proof that he had a strong work ethic is obvious due to his promotion to "overseer" (39:4). As we noted earlier, it was the presence of God that went with Joseph that made his situation in slavery better than his brothers' situation in freedom. But were the brothers really free? Free of guilt? Free of shame?

God's presence turned Joseph's prison into a palace. Yet, as we will see in today's reading, Joseph's time in the palace was short-lived.

Read Genesis 39:6b-20. Contrast Potiphar's wife's conduct with Joseph's.

Discuss the ways of Potiphar's wife and the steps she took in her evil plan for tempting Joseph.

List the four ways Joseph acted in the time of temptation. Support your answer with these verses.

This passage says that Joseph was not only godly in heart but also attractive and pleasant to the eye. Potiphar's wife noticed Joseph and desired him (v. 7). Herein lay the problem. The eye! It all began with a glance that turned into a stare. For her, Joseph was so much eye candy. But was this eye candy sweet, or sour?

Read Luke 11:34-36. Explain the function and purpose of the eye.

Many of us ruin our lives because we don't guard our eyes. We see that awful reality most vividly expressed by Potiphar's wife as she allowed darkness to invade her eyes, and her actions became unhealthy.

Today, what are some of the things we need to guard our eyes from?

Like a lamp shining on a path, the eyes let light enter our body and allow us to see obstacles that come in our way. When our eyes are healthy, they help us navigate our bodies toward a healthy lifestyle. When our eyes are clouded with junk we sometimes allow to creep in, our bodies will become depleted, and we'll waver in our ability to choose right from wrong.

What are some ways you can be deliberate about allowing light to enter your body?

What does Colossians 1:13 say about darkness?

Just as Joseph had clear eyes, he also had clear words for Potiphar's wife. Even though it was probably difficult for him as a buff, unmarried young man to resist the temptation, he did! He couldn't have been clearer in his refusal of her sinful suggestion. Because he respected his boss and his God, he resolved to say no to a very persistent woman. After all that, there was one last thing Joseph had to do—FLEE (v. 12)!

Potiphar's wife timed it well. She waited until the coast was clear and the house was empty. Just as Joseph's brothers committed their dastardly deed away from home, Potiphar's wife attempted to seduce Joseph in secret. The lesson for us is that seclusion can be deadly to our souls if it isn't prevented.

Also, she tempted Joseph after he had enjoyed time of success. He was prosperous in all that he did (v. 3), promoted to overseer (v. 4) and became popular and well- favored (v. 6). It was after all this had happened that Joseph was tempted (v. 7). Again, if success goes unchecked and we allow it to go to our heads, we make ourselves an easy target for temptation. Even though success isn't evil in itself and can be a result of God's blessing on us, just as Joseph experienced, it's just good to keep in mind that we can be the most vulnerable to temptation after a mountaintop experience.

What do the following verses say about fleeing?

1 Corinthians 6:18-20

2 Timothy 2:22

It is not a sign of weakness to run from temptation. When tempted, you will want to make a quick beeline in the opposite direction. This is the most practical way to deal with temptation. Don't try to reason with it or explain why you cannot do it, but avoid all contact with it. Ask other godly people to hold you accountable. It's also a good idea to "burn all bridges" behind you, making it impossible for you to be tempted.

Even though things may have looked dim for Joseph when he was locked up in jail (v. 20), maybe, just maybe, it was the perfect place for him.

Why do you think this confinement could have been good for Joseph?

Joseph was able to stand tall, even in the face of adversity once again, because he had the right views about sin and his God. This sin would have severely fragmented his relationship with God, so he was unwilling to take that chance, even if it meant death, which was what he should have been granted by Egyptian law.[1] But Potiphar was gracious unto Joseph. Though stripped of his jacket once again (v. 12), as well as his status among men, Joseph was not stripped of his character, and he retained his status with God. Now, that's what counts.

Oh dear God, I so want to be more like Joseph in my approach to life and godliness. Help me when I am swayed by the world or others to turn away from You. Help me to focus on You and You alone—that I will not turn to the left or right, but will stay fully focused on You. Help me keep my eyes clear and full of light, and ferret out any darkness within me.

My son, give attention to my words;
Incline your ear to my sayings.
Do not let them depart from your sight;
Keep them in the midst of your heart.
For they are life to those who find them
And health to all their body.
Watch over your heart with all diligence,
For from it flow the springs of life.
Put away from you a deceitful mouth
And put devious speech far from you.
Let your eyes look directly ahead
And let your gaze be fixed straight in front of you.
Watch the path of your feet
And all your ways will be established.
Do not turn to the right nor to the left;
Turn your foot from evil.

(Proverbs 4:20-27 NASB)

[1]Holman Old Testament Commentary: Genesis (Nashville: Broadman & Holman, 2002), 323.

Day Three

You Can Be Triumphant Over Temptation

Aren't you thankful for the example of Joseph, who refused to compromise his moral standards? Potiphar's wife tried three different techniques to grab Joseph's attention in Genesis 39. "Lie with me" (v. 7) was the first request, the second request was to "lie beside her" (v. 10), and the third was to "just be with her" (v. 10). Each request became a little more enticing and less invasive, but if Joseph would have compromised in any of the areas of temptation presented before him, they all had the potential to end the same way—lying with her. Even though Potiphar's wife camouflaged each request, Joseph was able to see through the temptation. He realized that one cannot compromise with evil and come out victorious, triumphant, and righteous.

We are going to take this day to explore a big piece of Joseph's character, that of commitment and resistance. We may not read from Genesis today, but our reading will point to the life of our much-loved Joseph.

What do the following Scriptures reveal about temptation?

Mark 14:38

1 Corinthians 10:12-14

James 1:13-14

Even Jesus was tempted (Matthew 4:1), but without sin. Second Corinthians 5:21 says, "He made Him who knew no sin to be sin on our behalf, so that we might become the righteousness of God in Him." How thankful are you to know that we have a God who knows our weaknesses and temptations? He is a God who cares about the details of our lives. Even during the heartbreak we may be suffering through, He can sympathize with our distress.

Read Hebrews 4:14-16 and describe the comfort you gain from it.

Let's take a moment and discover how we can draw near to God (Hebrews 4:16).

If we take the following steps from James 4, we will have a better chance of defeating the temptations in our lives.

Read James 4:7-10 and list what each verse encourages us to do in the process for defeating temptation.

Step One (v. 7)

Step Two (v. 7)

Step Three (v. 8)

Step Four (v. 8)

Step Five (v. 9)

Step Six (v. 10)

If any, which of these steps do you find difficult to carry out? Why?

I like to call this portion of Scripture the "C" factor: Commitment (steps 1 and 2), Cleansing (steps 3 and 4), and Contrition (steps 5 and 6). If we continually refresh our minds with these steps, we will be more likely to leave the temptations behind us. My pastor, Larry Burd, puts it like this: Give In, Get Close, Clean Up, and Get Down.

James 4:7-10

Give In

Get Close

Clean Up

Get Down

Yes, my sweet sisters, if we keep Jesus at the forefront of our minds, commit our life to Him and His control, take a stand against the Devil, desire a pure life, have a contrite spirit, and bow down before a holy God, He will make a way through the desert for us.

Just as Joseph's response to temptation was "no" the first time and "no" the second and third time, so should our response be when we're faced with temptation. We also should adopt his thought process: "How can I do this great wickedness, and sin against my God?" (Genesis 39:9). The honor of God was the great motivator for Joseph's purity.

Oh, that we would emulate Joseph's character, which is a vital factor to living a victorious and free life in Christ.

Ladies, there is freedom in restriction. Restriction will keep us safe and secure in the Father's hand. Sometimes we don't like or heed the restrictions because we think we can withstand temptations on our own. May it never be! We are too weak in our flesh to fight the battle by ourselves. Instead, we must allow God to fight the battle for us. So stand firm and let Him fight for you (Exodus 14:14).

I sure wish I had learned this lesson earlier in my life. How about you?

Some of you may be thinking, Well, good for Joseph. He provides a compelling example for sexual resistance, but I was not that strong. What if you have fallen into some sort of temptation? Perhaps it wasn't sexual temptation, but another form. Everyone has succumbed to temptation at some point because only Jesus has been tempted, yet without sin.

1 Corinthians 6:9-11. What comfort do you receive from verse 11?

Washed! Sanctified! Justified! Being cleansed by the blood, made holy by God, and declared righteous frees us from the rejection we have experienced as sinners. Oh yes, there is a part we must play. We must live out this special relationship by making sure we break all connections that lead us to sin.

Finish today's lesson by reading Psalm 51 with a heartfelt call after God.

Be gracious to me, O God, according to Your lovingkindness;

According to the greatness of Your compassion blot out my transgressions.

Wash me thoroughly from my iniquity

And cleanse me from my sin.

For you know my transgressions,

And my sin is ever before me.

Against You, You only, I have sinned

And done what is evil in Your sight,

So that You are justified when You speak

And blameless when You judge.

Behold, I was brought forth in iniquity,

And in sin my mother conceived me.

Behold, You desire truth in the innermost being,

And in the hidden part You will make me know wisdom.

Purify me with hyssop, and I shall be clean;

Wash me, and I shall be whiter than snow.

Make me to hear joy and gladness,

Let the bones which You have broken rejoice.

Hide Your face from my sins

And blot out all my iniquities.

Create in me a clean heart, O God,

And renew a steadfast spirit within me.

Do not cast me away from Your presence

And do not take Your Holy Spirit from me.

Restore to me the joy of Your salvation

And sustain me with a willing spirit.

Then I will teach transgressors Your ways,

And sinners will be converted to You.

Deliver me from bloodguiltiness, O God, the God of my salvation;

Then my tongue will joyfully sing of Your righteousness.

O Lord, open my lips,

That my mouth may declare Your praise.

For You do not delight in sacrifice, otherwise I would give it;

You are not pleased with burnt offering.

The sacrifices of God are a broken spirit;

A broken and a contrite heart, O God, You will not despise.

By Your favor do good to Zion;

Build the walls of Jerusalem.

Then You will delight in righteous sacrifices,

In burnt offering and whole burnt offering;

Then young bulls will be offered on Your altar.

Day Four

Keeping in the Presence of God

Okay, let's return to Genesis 39 and pick up the story with Joseph in confinement. We know that Joseph prospered by God in Potiphar's house and was put in charge. Now we will see how he prospers once again and is put in charge a second time. Joseph realized that his allegiance to God was the first requirement to become an ideal leader. In the pit he had to die to family, and now we see him in prison dying to reputation.[1]

Does this make you wonder if obedience to God pays?

What are your thoughts about this? Why or why not?

Sometimes obedience to God does not reap benefits immediately. Christ obeyed and was crucified; Paul obeyed and was put into prison, and even stoned; David obeyed and ran for his life; Joseph obeyed and was jailed. But eventually their obedience would pay off, for God never disappoints those who follow Him. Erwin Lutzer says, "The higher the cost of our obedience, the more glorious His approval and eventual rewards."[2]

Whether Joseph received benefits in this life or not is not the point. The point is that he was training for the world to come (heaven), and he kept that at the forefront of his mind. Joseph trusted that he would be adequately compensated in the life to come.

Read Genesis 39:20-23.

What important earthly things do you think Joseph lost when he was thrown in jail (v. 20)?

What repeated phrase do you see from this portion of Scripture regarding Joseph?

What was committed into Joseph's care?

Joseph paid a high price for purity. Although it was great, it was worth the cost. The opposite of purity is impurity, and the cost of impurity is far greater.

Joseph paid a high price for purity. Although it was great, it was worth the cost. The opposite of purity is impurity, and the cost of impurity is far greater. Even though Joseph was innocent, his reputation was scarred, his job lost, and the comforts of a warm, comfortable home replaced with the cold, bare floors of a dungeon. He lost his freedom, but he found favor with God, who raised him up once again to a leadership role.

Read 1 Peter 2:18-23.

What do these verses say about suffering unjustly?

How did this play out in Joseph's life?

How might it play out in your life today?

Most biblical scholars and commentators agree that Potiphar, the captain of the bodyguard (v. 1) as well as the chief jailer (v. 22), did not believe that his wife's tale about Joseph's seduction was true. The law of the Egyptians would have been extreme regarding adultery, so casting the offender into prison was a relatively light penalty. Verse 19 says that Potiphar burned with anger, but it neglects to say against whom the anger was directed. Was it directed toward Joseph, or his wife? You tell me.[3]

We have already established that Potiphar knew that God was with Joseph, so he made him overseer of the household. Now we read that Potiphar (chief jailer) made Joseph responsible for all the prisoners.

At first glance, it may appear to you that what happened to Joseph placed him at a great disadvantage. But when the Lord is with you, He can turn around any situation to His advantage.

John Butler astutely noted, "Our problem today is that we are more concerned about keeping out of the prisons of men than we are about keeping in the presence of God."[4]

> *"Our problem today is that we are more concerned about keeping out of the prisons of men than we are about keeping in the presence of God."*
> ~ John G. Butler

How would you respond to the statement above? Share in your own words what it means to you.

> *You adulterous people! Do you not know that friendship with the world is enmity with God? Therefore whoever wishes to be a friend of the world makes himself an enemy of God.*
>
> (James 4:4 ESV)

Read James 4:4.

What does this verse say about being friends with the world?

Read these Scriptures and discuss what you learned from them about the presence of God.

Psalm 42:4-5

Psalm 95:1-5

Hebrews 9:24

Unlike Joseph, we can water down our convictions, compromise our beliefs, or take part in questionable activities—all in order to avoid rejection from this world. But actually, wouldn't it be better for us to lose everything so that we can continue to stay in close fellowship with God? Staying in His presence daily is what allows us to move forward in our daily activities with strength and power beyond our own abilities.

Now, let's get practical. Besides the reality that God was with Joseph, what do you think Potiphar and the other higher-ups of the prison may have witnessed in Joseph's character that they did not see in the others?

These are just a few ideas that came to my mind, which I aspire to adopt as part of my life.

1. **Be good at what you do.** Just as Joseph followed through with the daily tasks involved with watching over the prisoners, so should we also take our responsibilities seriously.
2. **Step forward.** Volunteer for that "not so glamorous" job with willingness and an enthusiastic attitude.
3. **Promote the success of others.** When you see someone doing a good job, encourage them and acknowledge their contributions. Give credit where credit is due. Get more excited about what others are doing rather than what you are doing (Philippians 2:3-4).
4. **Be reliable.** You will never be perfect. But if you're a person who's capable, willing, and honest, you will be respected. Be the first to acknowledge your shortcomings and learn how you can improve.

I so wish I could be in your small group to hear your thoughts and ideas. Today's lesson encourages me to live out the same responsible, committed, and devoted life that Joseph did. Like him, I desire to have great zeal for God, no matter what the physical cost may be. Then, just as with Joseph, days of refreshment will come in His perfect timing.

[1]Erwin Lutzer, Keep Your Dream Alive: Lessons from the Life of Joseph (Grand Rapids, MI: Kregel Publications. 2003), 55.
[2]Ibid.
[3]John G. Butler, Joseph: The Patriarch of Character (Clinton, Iowa: Regular Baptist Press, 1993), 71.
[4]Ibid. , 76.

Day Five

Circumstances Shouldn't Imprison Our Hearts

So, do you think Joseph's dreams were shattered? His jealous brothers thought so when they sold him into slavery. They thought those dreams were over. Done. History. As a result of his imprisonment due to the false accusations of Potiphar's wife, Joseph also probably wondered if his dreams would ever be fulfilled. We have the privilege of unfolding the dream God had for Joseph—a dream of honor and respect. There was a divine purpose in all of it: "They afflicted his feet with fetters, he himself was laid in irons; until the time that his word came to pass, the word of the Lord tested him" (Psalm 105:18-19). Psalm 105 is a psalm about Israel's history, and this particular portion relates to Joseph. God indeed was testing him. Yet even though Joseph was at the lowest point of his life, he vividly took the high road and rose above the accusations and humiliation.

Read Genesis 40:1-8.

Who is placed in the care of Joseph? Why?

What did each man have?

What was Joseph's response?

From Genesis 39, we learn that Joseph was put in charge of those who were held in prison. Today, we meet two new prisoners—the baker and the cupbearer. These were two very important positions within the Pharaoh's court. The (chief) baker was more than just a pastry chef. He actually supervised all that went on in the kitchen. But what exactly does the chief cupbearer do? He was the official who would serve the king his drink, but only after he tasted it first to make sure it was safe for consumption. He watched over the king to make sure he was not poisoned.[1]

Even though we don't exactly know why these officials were thrown into confinement, we can only assume that the king was offended by them and there was a reasonable suspicion of guilt, so further investigation was needed (v. 1). Little did they know whom they would meet while in prison and the impact Joseph would make on their lives and vice versa.

"Some people live in a palace with their hearts in a prison; others live in prison with their hearts in a palace."

~ Erwin W. Lutzer

What we do know is that Joseph was aware of his surroundings and those under his care. He could tell that the two men were downcast and sad. Although he was in prison, Joseph had authority over his own heart. He knew that no one could make him angry, hateful, or discouraged except himself. But instead of focusing on his own pain, Joseph was watching out for the well-being of others.

In the same way, circumstances don't have such power unless we allow them to consume us. Circumstances should not imprison the human heart.

According to Mark 12:28-31, what are the two greatest commands?

Is God calling you back to Himself to watch over the well-being of another? How will you answer that call?

Each major shift in Joseph's life is preceded by a pair of dreams: the two dreams that gave Joseph hope and angered his brothers; the dreams of the baker and the cupbearer, the latter resulting in his release from prison; and a little later in our study, Pharaoh's dreams that elevated him to authority.

Let's consider the dreams of our two prisoners today.

Read Genesis 40:8-23.

What was Joseph's source of interpretation?

What is the cupbearer's dream and its interpretation? What was his outcome?

What is the baker's dream and its interpretation? What was his outcome?

What was Joseph's one request (v. 14)? What was his outcome (v. 23)?

For the first time we see Joseph show his hand to others regarding his unfair treatment: "For I was in fact kidnapped from the land of the Hebrews, and even here I have done nothing that they should have put me into the dungeon" (v. 15). But even with that revelation, Joseph was upright, respectful, and loyal. Joseph's jail time may have seemed like a lingering question mark to him, but from God's view, it was just a small piece to a heavenly puzzle.

Do you think it was hard for Joseph to see that God was present in his promotion as well as his demotion?

Here was Joseph's chance to pass go and get out of prison, but the chief cupbearer did not remember him (v. 23).

Have you ever felt forgotten by someone? If so, what was your response?

Even when we seem to be forgotten by others, we are not forgotten by God. We need to remember that His love for us outweighs the forgetfulness of man. And remember that from Day One this week we established that His thoughts of each one of us outnumber the grains of sand (Psalm 139:18).

How long, O Lord? Will you forget me forever?

How long will you hide your face from me?

How long must I take counsel in my soul

and have sorrow in my heart all the day?

How long shall my enemy be exalted over me?

Consider and answer me, O Lord my God;
light up my eyes, lest I sleep the sleep of death,
lest my enemy say, "I have prevailed over him,"
lest my foes rejoice because I am shaken.
But I have trusted in your steadfast love;
my heart shall rejoice in your salvation.
I will sing to the Lord,
because he has dealt bountifully with me.
(Psalm 13 ESV)

[1]Walk Thru the Bible: Joseph: The Power of Forgiveness (Grand Rapids, MI: Baker Publishing Company), 30.

WEEK THREE
VIDEO SESSION

PRINCIPLE 3:

“**RESILIENCE** comes when you no longer shrink back from the fear of man but live for the glory of God. 

Week Four

Day One
When the Time Is Right

Day Two
Shut the Door

Day Three
What's In a Name?

Day Four
An Old Dream Awakens

Day Five
A Second Go at It

Day One

When the Time Is Right

After the excitement of Pharaoh's birthday (40:20), when the chief butler (cupbearer) left prison and was reunited with Pharaoh, Joseph must have entered another dark period, if not the darkest of times. I imagine every day that a message arrived from Pharaoh, Joseph probably thought, This is the day—this is the day for my freedom. This is the day the cupbearer remembered to share what I did for him with Pharaoh. But no. Two years have passed as we continue to study the story of Joseph.

The same can happen to us, can't it? We expect the destiny to which we feel God has called us should happen immediately. Instead, what we hoped for becomes delayed. Someone forgets about us or a life-altering interruption detours our plans. What then?

Needless to say, there were times when my response was not very "Joseph-like." Was yours?

Now that we have studied part of Joseph's life, look back and think about the responses you've made to the unexpected detours in your own life's journey. Were your responses always the correct ones?

What do you believe about God's involvement in your life during those times?

How likely are you to thank God while you're waiting and trusting Him for His timing?

Is it possible to get tomorrow's perspective into our minds today? If so, how?

Let me share God's perfect timing with you through a learned lesson from my life. I hope this personal story encourages you to know that God sees the bigger picture and His timing is always right. This is an excerpt from my book, Road Trip.

In 1996, while sitting in the audience listening to the speakers at a Women of Faith event in my hometown, the words of a counselor who cared for me in a psychiatric hospital for three years ran through my mind: "Someday you will be sharing your experience with others." It was at that event I felt God calling me into a teaching/speaking ministry.

I didn't share this with anyone but my mother-in-law, who attended the conference with me. Even during my battle with Cushing's syndrome, I knew there was more to life than "just" surviving. I felt that God may use my story in a way that would encourage others.

At the time it was hard to understand God's will in it all, and even when I felt God's call, I didn't know what it was going to look like. Yet I still trusted Him with the outcome, or did I?

Although I felt God's call on my life in 1996, it was a twelve-year wait until I received my first invitation to share at another church. Honestly, there were times I wondered why. Why God, have You not opened the door yet? But during the twelve-year preparation, I would feverishly immerse myself in God's Word through multiple Bible studies, as well as work in various ministries. Each experience built on the previous one and prepared me for the open door God called me to enter many years ago.

There were times I felt discouraged that God didn't move a little faster in the process. I wanted to hurry Him along. Does this resonate with anyone?

But through a tough lesson, God wanted me to be willing to speak to one woman, not a multitude of women. You see, what God wanted and what I thought were very different. Humbled by a song I was listening to while waiting to pick up my then preschooler, God spoke to my heart, "Are you willing to speak to one person?"

When I finally bent my knee to His plan and became willing to speak to that one person, God began His plan, not mine. What I thought would be a call to reach multitudes, God meant for an audience of one. Likewise, at times you may wonder, Is this what God wants from me?

His calling on my life seemed to take longer to develop than I anticipated. Yet, through the waiting, I came to know God in a deeper way. He showed me more about Himself, and I realized that this preparation time was necessary for this season of my life.

If I had stepped ahead of God, it would have been a complete wreck. I would definitely not have been prepared.

Just like Joseph, you may be waiting and hoping for something to take place, but it has not yet come to fruition. Maybe, just maybe, you are not ready. Maybe God is still preparing you and teaching you so that when He does open the door, you will be more prepared. Most likely, if Joseph had been promoted when he was twenty years old, he might have been proud, domineering, and unsympathetic. If he would have been exalted then, he may have arrogantly thought that it was due to his own superior talents . . . . Wow!

What does James 4:10 say about exaltation?

For two years Pharaoh's chief butler forgot about Joseph. God allowed this because the time for Joseph's exaltation had not yet come. THEN God caused Pharaoh to dream. Yes, more dreams to unfold.

Read Genesis 41:1-16.

Explain dream # 1 (vv. 2-4).

Explain dream #2 (vv. 5-7).

What important event happened in verses 9-16?

Again we see a dream repeated twice, which confirmed its importance. Without help from the "hocus-pocus" attempts by the magicians of Egypt, Pharaoh knew there was a missing piece to the puzzle. Finally the chief butler came through. THEN he remembered Joseph (v. 9).

How was Joseph's response to Pharaoh (v. 16) different from his response to his brothers (37:6)?

What might have changed his attitude?

Do you think that Joseph could have been content with his role in prison? Two years had already passed, and the situation still hadn't changed. Needless to say, it was a wonderful day when Joseph, now thirty years old, shaved his Hebrew beard and changed into suitable clothing for his presentation before the king. He knew to whom he must give the glory as he answered Pharaoh, "I cannot do it, but God will give Pharaoh the answer he desires."

Read Philippians 4:12-14.

What is the "learned secret" by Paul? Do you think this is the same "secret" Joseph learned as well? Why?

Write out 1 Timothy 6:6-8.

Oh, that we would learn this lesson in our own lives—to be content despite our external circumstances and realize that our strength comes from Christ, who can do all things.

Trust Him with the outcome. Arise, and let the Christ in you shine through. He knows when the time is right!

Day Two

Shut the Door

Today's lesson comes from yesterdays quote: Trust Him with the outcome. He knows when the time is right!

We have watched Joseph silently serve over the last thirteen years, and now his life is going to take a turn toward a higher calling. He will still serve but with greater power and more of an authoritative voice. His initial dreams will now begin to take shape because the Almighty God has not forgotten him. We are unfolding the chain of events, along with the various strands of human experiences, in such a way that the pieces of his dream will come together.

Read Genesis 41:17-46.

What dream do you see repeated in verses 17-24?

Why do you think Pharaoh received two dreams?

What was the meaning of the two dreams (vv. 25-32)?

Joseph added, "It is as I have spoken unto Pharaoh: God has shown to Pharaoh what He is about to do" (v. 28). The repetition of the dreams for Pharaoh meant the matter was determined by God, and He would quickly bring it to pass. The matter was certain, so there was no room for another meaning.

Do you wish at times that you knew what God had planned ahead for you? Why or why not?

There were times I wished He had revealed what was ahead of me; but then, when I came through those circumstances to the other side, I was glad I didn't know the future that lay before me. Yet, in the case of Joseph and Pharaoh, their pre-knowledge greatly assisted them in the preparation for a fourteen-year situation. They were able to develop a plan and then execute it.

Sometimes we miss God's plan because we are too busy talking to Him, rather than listening to Him. We go into our quiet time with "this and that" on our minds and don't give God a chance to reveal Himself to us. God desires for us to come away with Him to that secret place, not just to present our requests, but to listen to Him. He wants us to listen to what His Word is speaking to us.

I recently heard of women attending a silent retreat, an event during which there is no talking but just meeting quietly with God. My first thought was, I don't think I could do that. But after further research, I have to reconsider. This might be just what is needed for us. Let's start each day by first meeting with Him and trying to be silent before Him. Waiting upon God will change our agenda.

What does Matthew 6:6 say we should do when we meet with Him?

We can immediately be in the presence of God if we just shut the door. When we shut out the distractions of the outside world and just meet with God, He will speak truth into our lives. I know this can be difficult for many of us in today's hurried world, but here are some ways that might help us begin or revive our time with God.

Circle the areas below in which you may need to take action:

- Decide what time of day works for you.
- Create your own secret place with God.
- Choose a Bible version that is easy for you to understand.
- Initially set realistic goals of how much you will read.
- Keep a journal for your thoughts.
- Regard your time with God as special time to cultivate your friendship with Him.
- Ask God to speak with you.

Don't become so regimented that you won't allow circumstances and seasons of life to change up your day. Try to be flexible when you approach a new adventure or change of situation. Sometimes I find myself multitasking when I meet with God. I infringe on my quiet time with my preparation of a Sunday school lesson or Bible study. I soon realized that when I was doing this, I was cheating myself and God. I was becoming an expert at serving God rather than "just being" His friend.

What distracts you when you meet with God?

My biggest distraction during my quiet time recently has been my ministry. At first, I didn't want to address that issue because I thought the two ran together—but no. I've discovered that spending quiet time with God and devoting attention to His Word allows me to "do" ministry because I can apply what I hear from God to my ministry. Sometimes I mix and match the two, and it comes out all scrambled.

In my case, I had to change the place where I meet with God. I found a place where there are no books, laptop, or to-do lists—a place where there's just me, God, and His Word (and, of course, a notepad to write what I hear from Him). After my quiet time, then I can go on to do my ministry tasks for the day.

Okay, sorry for the bunny trail, but it was just what we needed to hear.

Let's go back to the story of Joseph. Re-read Genesis 41:33-36.

What was Joseph's recommendation?

How did Pharaoh respond in verses 37-41?

Oh my, we need to catch our breath. This is all happening so fast for Joseph. Just minutes ago he was in prison, but now he's being elevated to second-in-command. Joseph was in stocks in the dungeon, but now Joseph is wearing Pharaoh's signet ring and is clothed in fine linen and gold (v. 42).

This promotion makes Joseph Pharaoh's right-hand man. Guess who's responsible to Pharaoh? Joseph's old boss (Potiphar), who is now beneath Joseph in the Egyptian hierarchy. Joseph could have used his influence to put Potiphar and his wife in their rightful place and cleared himself of all false accusations. Yet Joseph has learned not to take vengeance for himself but to allow God to have the final say.

Share the chain of events from Genesis 41:43-46 that took place in Joseph's life from this point forward.

Now take a look back to the point where we started back in Genesis 37 and recap the milestones in Joseph's life up to this point in Genesis 41.

Joseph was only seventeen years old when we met him back in Genesis 37, and now he is thirty years old in Genesis 47. Do you notice the hand of God on Joseph—how He has allowed all that adversity in his life to make him into the man He created him to be?

Sometimes we miss God's plan because we are too busy talking to Him, rather than listening to Him.

We are going to study further in the days ahead to see how God soon awakens an old dream within Joseph.

Day Three

What's In a Name?

One thing I kept thinking about at the end of yesterday's assignment was all that happened in Joseph's life from age seventeen to thirty. I then transferred that line of thought on reviewing my own life and all that has transpired—the good and not so good— and then recalling all that I learned from those experiences to make me the person I became. I remember turning thirty, joining my friends who had already reached that age milestone. I felt as if I had united with a special group of women as I headed into a new decade.

Take a moment and review the last thirteen years of your life. Where were you living? What were you doing? Who were you becoming? Can you look back on that time and observe the progression that has developed you into the person you are today?

After looking back at the past thirteen years of your life, list the attributes you see in yourself and the lessons you have learned. Describe yourself in terms of the person you are still becoming.

All that we've been and all that we are becoming involves God's plan unfolding before our very eyes. Our history is a vital piece of our future—a big part of who we become. It is important to take a look back because it can encourage us, even though sometimes it can also be a painful reminder of how far we have come. At any rate, we need to embrace the individual journey that God has allowed each of us to walk.

I wonder what Joseph's thoughts were when he looked back at his life experiences. As Joseph reflected on his life, he must have smiled about the better days ahead. Thankful that the dark days were disappearing, he must have also rejoiced when God rewarded him for his righteousness. He would once again be viewed as the prince in the palace. The new beginning for Joseph was Pharaoh's belief in him (41:37-41), but what Pharaoh really believed in was the God who was in Joseph.

Let's look back on the homes that Joseph supervised.

Read the following Scriptures and match them with the elevation of Joseph:

Genesis 37:3	His father Jacob's house
Genesis 39:4	Pharaoh's house
Genesis 39:22	Potiphar's house
Genesis 41:40	Prisoners' house

Joseph had proven his faithfulness in the three lesser assignments he had been given—overseeing his father's house, Potiphar's house, and the prison. Now he was assigned the greater task of overseeing Pharaoh's house and Egypt.

What does Luke 16:10 and Matthew 25:21 encourage us to be faithful in?

It doesn't appear that Joseph's elevation went to his head. Do you disagree? If so, why?

It is possible that Joseph's rigorous training of adversity and sorrow kept him level-headed. Also, he probably knew that at any moment his situation could change at the hand of another. He was able to encounter success because he left it in the hand of the Master, who watched over him.

Read Genesis 41:45-53.

What new name was Joseph given?

> *Joseph was able to encounter success because he left it in the hand of the Master, who watched over him.*

Zaphenath-paneah, Joseph's Hebrew name, has been given such meanings as "salvation of the world," "revealer of secrets," and "prince of the world." This name, which had so many powerful meanings, would certainly boost Joseph's reputation amongst the Egyptians. God had seen to it that Joseph had a name to match his character. And God will do the same for anyone who will stay faithful through trials and temptation. John G. Butler says, "Our responsibility is to take care of our character but let Him take care of the name and the reputation."[1]

> *"Our responsibility is to take care of our character but let Him take care of the name and the reputation."*
> ~ John G. Butler

Look up the following Scriptures and list the characteristic(s) for each verse that Christians should display.

Galatians 5:22-23

Romans 12:14

Colossians 3:13

1 Peter 5:3-5

1 Thessalonians 5:18

When you review these characteristics, you can see all of them displayed in Joseph. Joseph was a man of high character: he was responsible, content, forgiving, and so much more.

One day we will be given a new name (Revelation 2:17). What do you think yours might be?

How did the meanings of the names for Joseph's two sons exhibit his character before the Egyptian culture (41:51-52)?

By naming his sons as he did, Joseph proclaimed to the Egyptians that God had allowed him to forget all his troubles and be fruitful in the land of his afflictions. Joseph was a blessed man beyond measure in a place that once brought him suffering. God allowed Joseph to forget the pain of his past. Even though he may still have kept the memory of it, God removed the stinger from the harsh bite. In fact, Joseph did not allow his past to ruin his future because he realized that his God was bigger than both.

What painful memories are you having trouble with—to the point that you can't allow them to fade?

Be encouraged as you write out Joel 2:25.

Dear sister, allow God to be your great deliverer by trusting Him to bring about restoration.

[1]John G. Butler, Joseph: The Patriarch of Character (Clinton, Iowa: Regular Baptist Press, 1993), 106.

Day Four

An Old Dream Awakens

As we come to the end of Genesis 41, we see Pharaoh's dreams unfolding, as well as the hard work of Joseph paying off for Egypt and the surrounding countries. The plentiful food that was gathered and stored for seven years would now have to be distributed efficiently and strategically for the following seven years. In the words of Genesis 41:57, The people of all the earth came to Egypt to buy grain from Joseph, because the famine was severe in all the earth. For Joseph, an old dream awakens.

Read Genesis 42:1-9.

Who is reunited with Joseph and for what purpose?

What dream is awakened? Explain and supply verses.

Why was Joseph able to recognize his brothers, yet they weren't able to recognize him (vv. 7-8)?

Who do we see come back onto the scene but Joseph's brothers, minus Benjamin? Perhaps Joseph wondered if Benjamin had been eliminated because of their jealous anger. At any rate, they did not recognize Joseph the stranger. Why? Well, remember that when they sold Joseph into slavery, he was only a seventeen-year-old youth. They now see him as a thirty-seven-year-old man, cleanly shaven, ornately dressed, and versed in the Egyptian language. Moreover, as far as they were concerned, Joseph was a distant memory.

But on the other hand, it was easy for Joseph to recognize his brothers. How many "honest" brothers travel in a pack of ten—and all begotten by one father? Also, they must have resembled the young adult men Joseph left behind.

Continue reading Genesis 42:10-24.

What did Joseph accuse his brothers of being?

What was Joseph's plan for his brothers? Why do you think he kept Simeon behind in prison (v. 24)?

Joseph may have wanted to mirror the deeds done unto him by his brothers. So, with this probably in mind, he threw them in prison, which was a new experience for these Canaanite brothers. During these three days of confinement, they began to imagine what Joseph must have experienced back in Dothan. After Joseph brought them out of jail, not realizing that he could understand them without an interpreter, they confessed to one another, "Truly we are guilty concerning our brother, because we saw the distress of his soul when he pleaded with us, but we would not listen; therefore this distress has come upon us" (v. 21).

What emotion did Joseph show after he heard their confession (v. 24)?

Joseph was possibly smitten with mercy because he saw the beginning of the work of God in their hearts as they confessed their crime to one another. However, he likely felt that more atonement on their part should be made for their evil deeds. Changing his strategy, Joseph decided to keep Simeon, one of the cruelest among the brothers (34:25). He bound him in prison until the others returned.

Look up the following Scriptures. For each one, explain why confession is good for the soul.

Psalm 32:1-4

Psalm 66:17-19

Before seeing the nine brothers off on their journey back to their father, Joseph gave orders to have their bags filled with grain, along with the money they paid for the grain (vv. 25-26).

What was the response from the brothers upon opening one of the sacks (vv. 27-28)?

For I cried out to him for help,
praising him as I spoke.
If I had not confessed the sin in my heart,
the Lord would not have listened.
But God did listen!
He paid attention to my prayer.

(Psalm 66:17-19 NLT)

Understandably, the brothers only saw the gruff actions of an unkind man, which brought about their trembling. What they were yet to discover was Joseph's tender heart of compassion that lay under the surface. They only saw his rough hands, yet they did not see his loving tears. But Joseph's plan seemed perfect. Not only would it bring Benjamin to Egypt, but it would also measure the love of his brothers.

Let's close today's lesson with these thought-provoking questions: How much of this experience do you think was used to test his brothers' repentance? Or was it merely an opportunity to test Joseph's ability to forgive?

"The best test of repentance is to see how a person behaves when put in the same situation that led to his or her sin, so arranging an opportunity to betray the newly favored son will determine whether his brothers have changed."[1]

Have you ever been put in this position? Did you pass the test?

Now, you may have learned a hard lesson in your lifetime, but I hope when you're re-tested that you pass with flying colors, and come out holy, blameless, and beyond reproach (Colossians 1:22).

[1]Walk Thru the Bible; Joseph: The Power of Forgiveness (Grand Rapids, MI: Baker Publishing Company, 2009), 44.

Day Five

A Second Go at It

Upon the brothers' return to their homeland, they discovered that not only did one brother have money in his sack, but all of them had received the payment for the grain back in their individual sacks. They became fearful about what would happen to them, as well as what already may have been happening to Simeon when Joseph heard about the money "stolen" by the non-paying culprits. Because the brothers didn't know that Joseph had ordered the sacks of money placed in their bags to test them, they may have thought that Simeon was surely lost forever—just as Joseph was.

Read Genesis 42:29-38.

What repeated lie did the brothers tell their father, Jacob?

How could the brothers claim to be honest while remaining silent about the same old lie they had kept for over twenty years? Were their hearts so hardened that they believed their own lie? This lie may have softened the blow for Jacob in his old age, but it grieved God. Or just maybe this lie haunted them every day of their lives. I don't know what went through their minds, but if they had sensitive hearts, they could have gone to their father with repentant hearts, begged for forgiveness, and accepted the consequences that came their way.

Has God ever convicted you of something that you were afraid to face the consequences for? You may be like these brothers, living with something that happened twenty years ago and afraid to face the fiddler. Yet what God wants from you is honesty. Remember, there is freedom when you're being honest before God. Whatever your past sin may be, just give it to Him. Talk with someone you trust. Get counsel so you can have a clear conscience and live an upright life before God and man.

Remember the story Jesus told about the younger brother who returned to his father in Luke 15 (better known as the Parable of the Prodigal Son)? Let's read Luke 15:11-15 with a fresh eye.

Read Luke 15:20. What was the father's response?

The father who had been watching and waiting received his lost son with open arms of compassion as he ran to greet him. Immediately the father turned to his servants and told them to prepare a giant feast in celebration.

That is the same with our loving God. He is watching and waiting for one lost woman to honestly come to Him with a contrite heart so He can lavishly love on her. So He can lavishly love on YOU!

What was Jacob's response to his sons' return in Genesis 42:36 and 38?

Why do you think Jacob's response was different from the prodigal son's father?

Jacob cried, *"All these things are against me."* Have you ever made the same lament?

How did God help you through it?

Meanwhile, back in Egypt, Joseph understood that reconciliation was based on trust. Before he could reveal himself to his brothers, he had to know what was in their hearts. Joseph had learned that reconciliation takes time and dreams are sometimes fulfilled in terms of years—and even possibly in future generations. In the same way, we may not see tomorrow, but we will need to entrust ourselves and our dreams to the One that holds tomorrow.

We may not see tomorrow, but we will need to entrust ourselves and our dreams to the One that holds tomorrow.

Fill in the blanks of Proverbs 3:5-6 (NASB).

___________ in the Lord with all your heart. And do not lean on your own understanding. In all your ways ____________________ Him, and He will make your paths straight.

Time passed. They had been in the famine two years (45:6). It was probably one year after their first visit to Joseph. It had been long enough for the amount of grain they brought back with them to be depleted. I am sure Simeon's hope of their return was waning as well. So much still had to happen before Joseph's dream would be fulfilled.

Read Genesis 43:1-14. Explain how each person played a part in fulfilling Joseph's dream.

Jacob (vv. 2, 11-13)

Judah (vv. 3-5, 8-10)

Just as on a chessboard, many pieces needed to fall into place, as we see by Judah's suggestion and Jacob's response. Jacob was forced to trust God when backed into a corner. So he permitted Benjamin to join his brothers at the second go-round of facing Joseph. Benjamin would be the eleventh brother to bow before him.

We will close today's lesson by seeing Jacob at his best as he commits his sons to God in prayer: "And may God Almighty grant you compassion in the sight of the man, so that he will release to you your other brother and Benjamin. And as for me, if I am bereaved of my children, I am bereaved" (v. 14).

The Hebrew word for God Almighty used in this Scripture is El-Shaddai. Shaddai is derived from the related word that means "mountain," thus portraying God as the overpowering Almighty One, standing on a mountain.[1]

Can you picture it now? Jacob was watching his ten sons leave his sight as they faded into the distance, all the while entrusting them into the mighty hands of God as He watches from a high mountaintop. Sometimes that is all we can do. When there is nothing else we can control, we need to let go and let God.

[1]The Ryrie Study Bible (Chicago: Moody Publishers, 1986; 1995), 74.

Week Four
Video Session

Principle 4:

The One Who **REDEEMS** also brings life.

Week **Five**

Day One

Patience Is a Virtue

Day Two

Continued Testing

Day Three

I Am Joseph

Day Four

The "Withon" Us God

Day Five

Arise and Move Out

Day One

Patience Is a Virtue

I just got off the phone with a dear friend. She asked me, "How can I pray for you with only two weeks of homework to go?" I said, "Pray that I'll keep the fire burning." Oh, that we would continue to look for ways for God to impart His Holy Spirit's fire into our hearts as we seek out His application for each one of us through the story of Joseph.

As I sat down to begin writing today's assignment, my cute-as-a-button golden-doodle dog, Murphy, put his head on my lap, wanting to get up on my chair. He likes to be as close to me as he can be. You can imagine what that looks like—Murphy curled up on the back of my computer chair with his body wrapped around me, which doesn't leave much room for me. All he wants is some lovin' and care.

Isn't that what our Heavenly Father wants from us—to wrap ourselves around Him so that He would increase as we decrease (John 3:30) and there would be nothing of us, but everything of Him? Let's commit to finishing these next two weeks with great resolve and desire to be as close as we can get to our God.

Over the next couple of days, we will see the feelings of closeness Joseph has for his brothers as he reveals himself at just the right moment—not a moment too soon. Again, God's timing will be perfect.

Read Genesis 43:15-24.

Who accompanies the brothers on the second trip back to Egypt?

What was Joseph's response?

Circle the emotion(s) that you see taking over Joseph's brothers?

Fear Panic Love Acceptance Paranoia Trust

Do you think Joseph thought about what his response would be to his brothers when they returned? He probably had a year to consider how he would receive them if they returned. Have you ever rehearsed a response in your mind to someone you needed to face? It can be all-consuming, and the anticipation can be even worse than the action. The brothers, under the direction of their father, knew it was necessary to present Joseph with a gift. But actually, Benjamin's presence was gift enough for Joseph.

Sometimes, that is all we have to give to another—our presence. No gift is necessary, and no deed matters. Your presence is all that's needed. Just the touch of your hand, the kiss of your lips, the warmth of a hug, or the whisper of love will be enough.

If you have read any of my other books, you know that I have a dear friend, Dora, who turns a hundred years old this year. I always go to her home on her birthday, which is also my anniversary date. Does it matter if I bring a gift? No. All that matters is that I care, I remember, and I love on her. Who is waiting to receive this from you? It takes no money, just time, which is precious and yields a lifetime of gratitude.

Read Genesis 43:23-24. What do these verses indicate that Joseph shared with his steward?

What was the steward's response?

The care from the steward exemplified grace and generosity. It could have been evidence that Joseph's character was rubbing off on an Egyptian man, and Joseph's God was becoming his God as well.

Continue reading from Genesis 43:26-34.

What part of Joseph's dream was fulfilled a second time in verse 26?

What emotion does Joseph show once again (v. 30)?

What does Psalm 56:8 say that God does with our tears?

What does Joseph do once again as he approaches his brothers (v. 31)?

It would have been so easy for Joseph to allow his emotions to control him and immediately throw his arms around his brother, Benjamin, and reveal himself to his brothers. But Joseph knew the time wasn't right yet. The virtue of patience was still needed. He wanted to see his brothers prove their character before he blessed them.

As women, sometimes we don't pass the test of patiently controlling our emotions. Instead, we often allow our emotions to be worn on our sleeves for all to see. This can get in the way

> *Patient waiting is a virtue that takes practice and is only learned by consciously instilling it within our spirit over and over. Be patient with yourself; it involves a lifetime of practice.*

of waiting on God's timing in a particular situation. There are times when I have wanted to just jump out of my skin with excitement over an upcoming event, so I have prematurely went ahead of God, only wishing later that I had waited it out. Patiently waiting is a virtue that takes practice and is only learned by consciously instilling it within our spirit over and over. Be patient with yourself; it involves a lifetime of practice.

Read the following Scriptures and discuss what each one says about self-control.

Proverbs 16:32

Galatians 5:22-23

Patience and self-control are listed among the fruit of the Spirit. So impatience can be considered a fruit of the flesh, and we shouldn't excuse it by saying, "It's just part of my personality." We must rather make a great effort to change ourselves from being impatient people to patient ones. John G. Butler says, "Emotions are not sinful in themselves; the sin is the failure to control them." Had Joseph not controlled his emotions, he would have spoiled everything by revealing himself too soon. By doing that, he would have never known for sure that his brothers had really changed.[1]

> *Better to be patient than powerful; better to have self-control than to conquer a city.*
>
> (Proverbs 16:32 NLT)

What did the seating look like as they dined together (v. 32)?

What was evident to the brothers as they sat down for their meal (v. 33)?

Do you see any signs of jealousy with the brothers as Benjamin receives, not double, but five times as much as the others (v. 34)? Explain your answer.

The brothers are back together, behaving in perfect order. They pass the second test of not acting harshly toward Benjamin because of the favoritism shown to him. There is indeed still hope for Joseph's siblings.

> *"Emotions are not sinful in themselves;the sin is the failure to control them."*
>
> ~ John G. Butler

The brothers and the Egyptians eat at two different tables because the Egyptians could not eat with foreigners. That was a cultural no-no, and if Joseph had violated this custom, it would have been detestable to all present. Joseph has his own table because he is a man in between two cultures—too high-ranking to eat with his own staff and too Egyptian (as far as anyone knows) to eat with Hebrews. Yet he represents what God has done with us by bridging the gap between the needs of his family and the provision God has planned for them. Essentially, he is a mediator between God and his chosen people.[2]

Does this sound like someone else from the Scriptures? Who?

Read 1 Timothy 2:5-6 and explain how Joseph symbolizes the greatest mediator of all.

> *For there is only one God and one Mediator who can reconcile God and humanity—the man Christ Jesus. He gave his life to purchase freedom for everyone. This is the message God gave to the world at just the right time.*
>
> (1 Timothy 2:5-6 NLT)

Joseph's life offers us a portrayal of God's grace as He came to our rescue through the sacrificial death of His Son, Jesus. Many people come to God just as Joseph's guilty brothers did, fearing the worst, only to be treated with great mercy by Him.

Charles R. Swindoll says, "Instead of being blamed, we are forgiven. Instead of feeling guilty, we are freed. And instead of experiencing punishment, which we certainly deserve, we are seated at His table and served more than we can ever take in."[3]

Dear sister, Jesus knew about your future sins before you were born and He died on the cross before you ever entered this world. So He took all your future sin upon Himself at the cross two thousand years ago. Now, please stop taking those sins back as if He never has forgiven them. You are forgiven, you are loved, and you are firmly in His grip.

[1]John G. Butler, Joseph: The Patriarch of Character (Clinton, Iowa: Regular Baptist Press, 1993), 124.
[2]Walk Thru the Bible; Joseph: The Power of Forgiveness (Grand Rapids, MI: Baker Publishing Company), 48.
[3]Charles R. Swindoll, Joseph: A Man of Integrity and Forgiveness (Nashville: Thomas Nelson, 1998), 132.

Day Two

Continued Testing

Joseph's brothers were now reunited. Simeon was back with them, and Benjamin was once again under their protection. Feeling pretty good about their visit with their still estranged brother, Joseph, they head home to Jacob with filled bags of grain, together as one unit. But would they remain together? How would they react to the continued testing brought their way once again? Let's continue to read this intriguing story with its many twists and challenges.

Read Genesis 44:1-12 and answer the following questions.

What did Joseph order his steward to do with his brothers' bags?

What position do Joseph's brothers take (v. 7)?

In whose sack was Joseph's favorite cup stashed?

Although accused of stealing Joseph's favorite cup, the brothers seemed pretty confident that they were innocent: Then they hurried, each man lowered his sack to the ground, and each man opened his sack (v. 11). I don't think they would have been in such a hurry to reveal the contents in their bags if they were guilty, do you?

Continue reading Genesis 44:13-34.

How was the brothers' response to Benjamin different, compared to their response to Joseph back in Genesis 37 (v. 13)? Did the brothers confess their sins?

Despite the certainty of Joseph's charge against them, they said in verse 9, "With whomever of your servants is found, let them die, and we also will be my lord's servants." They knew they were innocent of this accusation of stealing. Joseph's servant then slightly changed what the brothers said as he responded to them, "He whom is found shall be my slave, and the rest of you shall be innocent" (v. 10).

No death by the servant's hands would take place, so the brothers' attitude was the opposite of what it was with Joseph. If one brother had to return, they all had to return. This time they would not leave a younger brother to become enslaved in a foreign land. They were not going home to Jacob without taking his favorite son, Benjamin, with them.

According to verse 14, what added demonstration of honor did the brothers show Joseph?

Which brother steps forward to represent the clan? And what did he confess (v. 16)?

For the third time, the brothers found themselves not only bowing but now throwing themselves before Joseph. This is an act of humility and honor. Judah claimed the brothers' innocence in regards to the theft of the silver cup, yet he confesses a sin concealed to others, though known to God. It was brought to light as Judah began one of the noblest speeches in God's Word.

Re-read verses 19-34.

What does Judah proclaim to Joseph?

What is Judah's alternate plan (vv. 33-34)?

Judah, the brother who had suggested selling Joseph into slavery rather than killing him, now defends Benjamin. He stands in the gap for his father and begs Joseph to keep him there in place of his younger brother.

What was the test Joseph presented to his brothers? Did they pass the test?

How does this portion of Joseph's story apply to your own life? Are you like Joseph, remaining silent about a situation until the right time, while extending grace? Or are you on the receiving end, regaining trust from another person? Both positions take work and time, as well as power from a source greater than yourself. The Holy Spirit must be allowed to work in you to conform you to be more like Jesus. Through time, you can prove yourself to be trustworthy, while the other person extends the grace needed for this. But you may ask, "What if the other person doesn't extend grace?" Even if grace isn't extended by the other person, the only thing you can do is work on yourself and leave the rest in God's capable hands. Then He will work on the hearts of the others.

Do you find yourself like Joseph, extending grace to another? If so, how are you doing?

Or are you like Joseph's brothers, repentant and regaining trust from another? If so, how are you doing?

According to 1 Corinthians 15:9-10 and Colossians 1:29, whose power do you need to rely on?

For I am the least of the apostles, and not fit to be called an apostle, because I persecuted the church of God. But by the grace of God I am what I am, and His grace toward me did not prove vain; but I labored even more than all of them, yet not I, but the grace of God with me.

(1 Corinthians 15:9-10)

As you continue working on the area God is revealing to you, remember that progress is not accomplished by your own strength but rather by the strength provided by His saving grace. He will provide the power by which you can

For this purpose also I labor, striving according to His power, which mightily works within me.

(Colossians 1:29)

reach up to it. He asks nothing of you except your willingness. You supply the willingness; He supplies the power. Never fear that God's challenges are beyond you. They are beyond you only if you are unwilling to avail yourself of His power.[1]

Remember, sweet sisters, it's the vine that provides the power, not the branches!

For our last Scripture reading today, please read John 8:1-11 and answer the following questions.

What did Jesus do for the adulterous woman?

What was the woman's posture at the beginning of the story?

What was her posture at the end of the story?

What does Jesus say to her in verse 11? " ________________ sin no more."

Jesus can do the same for you: stoop down, write you a love letter, straighten your posture and your countenance, and then send you on your way. From now on, who will you be?

[1]Selwyn Hughes, "Every Day with Jesus: The Great Legacy," March/April 2014 (UK: CWR, 2014).

Day Three

I Am Joseph

After Judah's plea, the time had come. Joseph could no longer contain himself. Today, we are heading right into the climax of Joseph's life. I don't want to spoil it for you, so I'm going to ask you to read it for yourself right from the start. Amidst much anticipation, God will display His sovereignty to a watching family and listening country.

Read Genesis 45:1-15.

Share the dramatic details in your own words of Joseph's unveiling and how each one reacted (vv. 1-3).

Joseph

The brothers

Pharaoh's household

After all the incredible events that have led up to this point, with great anticipation Joseph reveals his identity to his brothers. "I am Joseph!" he says in the Hebrew dialect so his brothers would understand. There is no interpreter to explain Joseph's words except Joseph himself. These are some descriptions of the brothers' reactions: stunned (NLT); dismayed (NASB); terrified (NIV); and speechless (MSG). I am sure the brothers were excited to know that Joseph was alive, although they were also afraid. Joseph had the power to do with them as he wanted, but we will see his loving kindness displayed to them as he continues his unveiling.

Whose plan was it for Joseph to go to Egypt—his brothers' or God's (vv. 4-5, 7-8)?

Do you think it took Joseph twenty-plus years to see the revelation of God's plan? It was for this very moment that all the heartache, all the loneliness, and all the agony and wonder paid off. The dream given to him when he was seventeen years old was being fulfilled.

What do you think Joseph learned about God as he looked back over the past twenty-two years?

God's dreams are not always easy to accept because they often include many tears and sometimes rejection by others. Joseph also was learning a small dream can result in a big blessing. Little did he know that his dream would not only affect his family but the whole world. Indeed, no one but God can see the significance of one small dream.[1]

Share about an experience that you thought was insignificant but had profound implications later.

One cannot foresee the consequences that a single sin will produce—or the ministry that may evolve from that same dark time. Nor can we see the great blessing that will come from one act of righteousness. Sometimes you may even wonder why you were placed on this earth. Does your life mean anything to someone? Does what you do even matter?

While writing this Bible study, some of these very thoughts went through my mind as I spent many days with "myself." These thoughts didn't arise because of the actions of anyone. Instead, the Evil One was putting them in my mind, and I was dwelling on them. Then one day, after taking a short break and checking social media, the first thing that popped up on my Facebook feed was this: If you are breathing, God has a purpose for you. As long as you have breath, somebody needs what you have—your gifts, your talents, your love, your smile.

> *"If you are breathing, God has a purpose for you. As long as you have breath, somebody needs what you have—your gifts, your talents, your love, your smile."*
> ~Author unknown

Sister, your life does matter. You are significant. You are worthy. And God has a plan for you, plans for good and not disaster, to give you a hope and future (Jeremiah 29:11).

What does Joseph request of his brothers in verses 9-13?

How did Joseph further show his love to his brothers, according to verses 14-15?

What do you think their conversation might have sounded like as the brothers talked with Joseph after his unveiling (v. 15)?

Can you picture this scene in verses 14-15? Joseph was showing his love for Benjamin as he wept on his neck, and Benjamin reciprocated that same love back to Joseph as he wept on his neck, too. This is brotherly love at its best. Then, Joseph went over to his remaining brothers, kissed them, and wept "over" them. The brothers could have bowed down once again before Joseph in order for him to weep over them. Furthermore, in this split second, any of the appalling memories Joseph may have had seemed to dissipate with a kiss. With the ultimate act of kindness, Joseph forgave them.

As you look back over this story thus far, you're able to see a little clearer the hand of God upon Joseph. Now you can understand Joseph's response, "God sent me before you to preserve a remnant" (v. 7), which referred to what God told Abram in Genesis 15:13, "Your descendants will be strangers in a country not their own [Egypt], and they will be enslaved and mistreated four hundred years."

One last thing was still needed—the restoration of Joseph to his father, Jacob (v. 13).

Let's take the remainder of today's lesson to explore a statement made back in Week One: Many scholars will say that Joseph foreshadows the person, who altogether is lovely in character, Jesus Christ. I think this is a good time to shed light on this statement.

Read the following Scriptures and explain how Joseph's life foreshadows the role and ministry of Jesus.

Romans 11:25; Colossians 1:26-27

Matthew 23:37

Romans 11:26

Romans 11:1-5

Jeremiah 50:20

Joseph discovered that in the kingdom of God, the glory of the destination always outweighs the pain of the journey to get there.

~ Walk Thru the Bible

The events of Joseph's life foreshadow the role and ministry of Jesus in remarkable detail: redemption, forgiveness, and reconciliation. Just as Joseph's days were concealed from his brothers, so were Jesus' from the Gentiles. Both wept. Joseph preserved a remnant, and so would Jesus. Joseph forgave his brothers, just as Jesus would forgive Israel's rejection of Him. And just as God worked out ancient Israel's salvation through the treachery of Joseph's brothers (v. 5), he worked out the ultimate salvation of the human race through the Jews' treachery in killing the Messiah. Yes, we all agree that up to this point, Joseph lived a difficult life, which was ultimately worth the grief. He found God to be faithful in every trial and discovered that in the kingdom of God, the glory of the destination always outweighs the pain of the journey to get there.[2]

Great job today, ladies! Tomorrow we will see the final piece of the puzzle come together as we read about Jacob's reaction to Joseph's whereabouts.

[1]Erwin W. Lutzer, Keep Your Dream Alive: Lessons from the Life of Joseph (Grand Rapids, MI: Kregel Publications, 2003), 112.

[2]Walk Thru the Bible; Joseph: The Power of Forgiveness (Grand Rapids, MI, Baker Publishing Company, 2009), 8, 9, 54, 55.

Day Four

The "Withon" Us God

Nothing blesses my soul more than hearing good news from my husband, our daughters, or from family and dear friends. This is especially true when I know it's something they've been longing for. When the breakthrough comes, everything in me wants to bless them with words of encouragement or a small gift, or share their excitement with others. This is exactly what happens with Joseph and Pharaoh.

The news was heard! And heard it was. Pharaoh couldn't help but overhear the wailings of Joseph and the announcement to his brothers. Joseph once again is overseeing his household through the renewed relationship with his brothers. And then when the news was heard by Pharaoh, he was pleased and blessed them.

Is there something you are rejoicing over right now that deserves a blessing?

According to Genesis 45:16-23, how did Pharaoh instruct Joseph to bless his family?

Joseph's brothers had all they needed for their journey back to Canaan and then some, dressed in fashion, riding in style, and hauling an overflowing source of food. Imagine this sight as they trekked back to Canaan. Those they passed must have wondered who they were and how they had received all this food during this time of famine. I'm sure even the brothers were stunned over the abundance they received.

Have you ever received more than you expected from someone or from a particular situation? What did it look like?

What last command did Joseph give his brothers before they left for Canaan in verse 24?

I'm so glad when we find a little morsel like this in the Scriptures: "Do not quarrel on the journey." It keeps it real. I remember one night before my girls were heading back to college. They both attended the same school for two years, so it was nice they could travel together. But on this particular day, they had experienced a misunderstanding, so as they left, this caring mother said, "Please don't quarrel on your way back." Like any concerned mother, I wanted my daughters to love each other and realize they were the best friends each of them would ever have. And yes, the next day I followed up their ride with a letter stating this. Just keepin' it real . . . .

Even though Joseph spent a considerable time apart from them, he knew that there was probably still some of the old nature in them that could cause them to argue.

What do you think they could have argued over?

I so wish I could be sitting with you as you discuss this quarrelsome group of brothers. No matter what they talked about on their journey back to Canaan, however, they arrived safely at their father's door.

Read Genesis 45:25-28.

What did the brothers share with Jacob?

How did Jacob initially react to the news?

The message given to the brothers was the reason for their journey back to their father, and they delivered it in full: "They told him all the words of Joseph" (v. 27). They did not water the message down by changing or altering it in any way. This was probably a hard message for the boys to relay. It was humbling, to say the least. But it would have been worse for them if they had not declared the message.[1]

As believers, we sometimes might find it difficult for one reason or another to relay the message God gives us, but we must not hesitate to share it anyway.

What does Paul declare in Acts 20:27?

Read Matthew 5:14-16. What does it say is required of us?

What are some ways we hide that light today?

I don't think we intentionally set out to hide the light (Jesus Christ) that burns within us. A lot of times it's the subtle things that pass us by, such as those times we remain quiet when we should speak, go along with the crowd, deny the light, don't explain our light to others, or ignore the needs of others. When I first wrote this paragraph, I said, "I don't think we intentionally set out to hide the light (Jesus Christ) that burns withon us," and it auto-corrected the spelling to within us. But as I looked at it, the sentence made sense to me. We must have Jesus "withon" us as much as "within" us. He must be all over us if we expect a watching world to notice His presence and work in our lives. What is inside must be seen by those watching us. Psalm 34:5 says, "when you look to Him, you will be radiant, and your face will never be ashamed."

We must have Jesus "withon" us as much as "within" us.

Letting our "light shine before men" allows others to see our "good works," the beautiful transformation that the Lord has worked in us. It is the light of Jesus that shines through our cracks: the cracks of forgiveness, conviction, and redemption. To see the good works done by us is to see Christ in us. That's why Jesus says, "Let your light shine." It is something we allow the Lord to do in us and on us. It is God's light but our choice to hide it or let it shine. As Paul exhorts us, we must lay aside the deeds of darkness and put on the armor of light (Romans 13:12).

What is the purpose of letting your light shine, according to Matthew 5:16 and 9:8?

We allow God's light to shine through us so God will receive the glory. Our intent should be that in all we are and all we do, others may see God and "glorify [our] Father who is in heaven." It's not about us, but all about Him.

When was the last time you were awestruck by His glory?

But when the crowds saw this, they were awestruck, and glorified God, who had given such authority to men.

(Matthew 9:8 NASB)

Others were able to see the Almighty God "withon" Joseph through the wearing of the jacket, the demeanor of his stature, and the confidence in his speech due to the strong conviction that was within him.

[1]John G. Butler, Joseph: The Patriarch of Character (Clinton, Iowa: Regular Baptist Press, 1993), 143.

DAY FIVE

Arise and Move Out

Have you ever heard such shocking news that you stood amazed until you actually saw the evidence? This is what happened with Jacob. It was only when he saw the wagons coming from a distance that Joseph had sent to carry him back to Egypt that the spirit of Jacob was revived (45:27). Revival can come in one word.

Revival can come in one word.

Read Psalm 119:25, 50, 149, and 156.

What revives the psalmist?

What name is Jacob called in Genesis 45:28?

Jacob now had a little kick left in his old body when he heard his son, Joseph, was alive. Believing the promise that God would be with him and would keep him on his journey (28:20), Jacob (Israel) said, "It is enough that Joseph is alive." He was thankful that God remembered His promise and fulfilled it through his much-loved son. Israel had already lived up to his name, prevailing with men and God (32:28), and now he prepared to go forth to Egypt to visit Joseph before he died. What a day of rejoicing that must have been!

Today, we will read all of chapter 46 at one sitting, so please take the time now to read it. There are many names listed throughout this chapter. All the names are very important in the future life of the nation Israel. Please don't skip over them. (Okay, you can skim them, but please don't miss the dynamics of the father/son embrace.)

Read Genesis 46:1-34.

After leaving Canaan, where was Israel's (Jacob's) first stop? What did he offer there (v. 1)?

What command and promise was given to Jacob (vv. 2-4)?

From the following Scriptures, discuss the significance of Beersheba.

Genesis 22:19

Genesis 26:23-25

This place, Beersheba, was a place of great significance in the lives of Abraham, Isaac, and now Jacob. It was a place of importance, a place of intimacy, and a place of direction.

In *Secrets of the Secret Place*, Bob Sorge writes, "Intimacy precedes insight. Passion precedes purpose. First comes the secret place, then comes divine guidance. God doesn't simply want to get us on the right path. He wants to enjoy you throughout your journey . . . . God's primary desire is not that you discover His will and walk in it; His primary desire is that you draw near to Him and come to know Him."[1]

While Jacob met with God in the intimate place of Beersheba, he was encouraged. You witness Jacob exercising his faith at Beersheba as he prepares to leave the land of promise and head to Egypt, a country despised by the Jewish people. Jacob realized he was not alone. He also knew that God would make something out of his life if he would remain faithful to Him.

Is there something you need to remain faithful to God for?

You have heard that God doesn't call the equipped; He equips the called. That is exactly what is happening in this story. The message here shows God will be there to love you and guide you to accomplish great things. Bob Sorge says, "Your worst days are never so bad that you are beyond the reach of God's grace. And your best days are never so good that you are beyond the need of God's grace."[2]

> *"Your worst days are never so bad that you are beyond the reach of God's grace. And your best days are never so good that you are beyond the need of God's grace."*
> ~ Bob Sorge

It was now time for Jacob to arise and move out in action (46:5)—to step out of the protected place of Beersheba and put action to all that he had received from his time spent with his Father. He took everything with him, from livestock to family, and set on his journey. Genesis 46:8-27 lists the members of Jacob's family who went with him.

How many members of Jacob's family traveled with him from Canaan (v. 27)?

Is God asking you to arise and move out to accomplish a certain mission? What will that look like?

Next stop, Goshen. Re-read Genesis 46:28-30 and explain the father/son reunion in your own words.

Although Joseph was of high position and power, instead of waiting for his father to come and bow before him, he did the opposite. He went to Goshen to meet his father, Israel. As soon as he appeared before him, he fell on his face and wept on his neck a long time (v. 29). In the Hebrew, the word "presented" (ESV) or "appeared" (NIV) in our text is generally used only regarding the appearance of God.[3] But here the word is used to express the glory in which Joseph went to meet his father. No words were spoken at this moment, for words could not express the depth of gratitude and love within their hearts. Then the words, "Now let me die," broke the silence.

Close out today's lesson by looking at Joseph's plan with regards to Goshen. What were the brothers instructed to say to Pharaoh when asked about their occupation (vv. 31-34)?

Tomorrow we will see if the brothers were obedient to Joseph's instruction . . . Stay tuned!

[1]Bob Sorge, Secrets of the Secret Place: Keys to Igniting Your Personal Time with God (Lee's Summit, MO: Oasis House, 2005).
[2]Ibid.
[3]Butller, John G. Joseph , The Patriarch of Character. Clinton, Iowa: Regular Baptist Press, 1993. 147.

WEEK FIVE
VIDEO SESSION

PRINCIPLE 5:

"SOMETIMES WE WILL NEED TO GO TO A HARD PLACE BEFORE **RECONCILIATION** HAPPENS—A HARD PLACE WITH OURSELVES OR WITH OTHERS."

Week Six

Day One

A Sojourner's Blessing

I wish I could put into words the feelings I am experiencing as we embark on our last week of study. For more than two years I have been excited about studying Joseph with you. Multiple books and commentaries sat on my bookstand, and each time I would look at them, I felt such a strong pull to begin. Yet I knew God was telling me to wait until His timing was right. As I mentioned in the opening day of our study together, I came to love Joseph nearly a decade ago, and now through this in-depth study, I love him even more. I hope you have learned as much as I have and that you are able to apply the lessons of Joseph to your own life in tangible ways. For some of you, this may be the first time your Bible has been cracked open to the pages of the Old Testament. And others of you have read Joseph more times than you can count. Wherever you may have been at the start, we have all finished this journey together at the same place. Let's finish this study with as much devotion as we began it.

Read Genesis 47:1-12.

Who did Joseph present to Pharaoh first (v. 2)?

How did Joseph's brothers respond to Pharaoh (vv. 3-4)?

How did Pharaoh respond to Joseph (vv. 5-6)?

Curiosity is getting the best of me. How about you? I so want to know which five brothers were presented to Pharaoh. Was it Judah, who has become the face of the family; Benjamin, the youngest and most loved son; Reuben, the oldest; or the others we don't know much about? We will become more acquainted with them as we look at the blessing that Jacob, at the end of his life, speaks over each one in Genesis 49.

Did you catch the brothers' response in Genesis 47:4? "We have come *to sojourn* (ESV, emphasis mine), or "We have come *to live here for a while*" (NIV, emphasis mine). The length of time Jacob's family probably planned to stay in Egypt were the remaining five years of the famine. Little did they know the words spoken to Abraham in Genesis 15:13, "Your descendants will be strangers in a land that is not theirs, where they will be enslaved and oppressed for four hundred years," were about to begin with them.

What do the following Scriptures say about us as foreigners?

Ephesisans 2:19

1 Peter 1:17

1 Peter 2:11

Have you ever thought that you would only be in a certain place for a short time but then realized God was settling you there for longer than you anticipated? Explain.

Now we come upon the presentation of Joseph's father to Pharaoh (47:7). Jacob, an old man, is wrinkled, and lame from his wrestling match with God (32:31). Pharaoh is dressed in his royal garb and Jacob in his peasant attire. Unashamed, Joseph doesn't hesitate to bring his father to Pharaoh.

What is Jacob's response when he meets Pharaoh in Genesis 47:7, 10?

Friends, this world is not your home, so don't make yourselves cozy in it. Don't indulge your ego at the expense of your soul. Live an exemplary life among the natives so that your actions will refute their prejudices. Then they'll be won over to God's side and be there to join in the celebration when he arrives

(1 Peter 2:11 MSG)

The statement where Jacob blessed Pharaoh with means "to endue with power for success, prosperity, fecundity, longevity, etc." Blessing is conveyed from the greater to the lesser, such as father to son, or king to subject. Jacob expresses faith in God's promises and acts on the promise that "all peoples on earth will be blessed through you and your offspring" (28:14).[1]

What do the following Scriptures say in regard to honor?

Exodus 20:12

Ephesians 6:2

What are some ways we can honor our parents today, whether we're young or old?

There is no doubt that Pharaoh received many blessings due to hosting Joseph in his land and his home. And Pharaoh acknowledged this blessing because he respected Jacob for reaching the age of a hundred and thirty, being Joseph's father, and professing his faith in God. After Jacob's blessing, Pharaoh told Joseph to settle his family in "the best of the land" (v. 11).

What did Joseph provide for his family in Genesis 47:12?

Let's backtrack. The nation of Israel was brought into Canaan originally by Abraham when he left Haran at the age of seventy-five (12:4-6). He then sojourned to Egypt because of a great famine. (Does this sound familiar?) After Abraham lied about Sarah being his sister, Pharaoh sent him on his way, so back to Canaan they went (13:12). When he left his father-in-law's house, Abraham headed for Canaan and made his home in Shechem, a small village in the land of Canaan. After the massacre in Shechem, Jacob moved his family about fifteen miles away, to Bethel, a city that is still a part of Israel (35:1).

The rest of the story we have already studied: the famine hit Jacob and his family, which forced them out of Canaan and back to Egypt. Israel's suffering was a part of God's divine plan, so eventually they would return to Canaan. I believe Jacob trusted in the promise given to his great-grandfather generations earlier. God said to Abram, "Know for certain that your descendants will be strangers in a land that is not theirs, where they will be enslaved and oppressed four hundred years. But I will also judge the nation whom they will serve, and afterward they will come out with many possessions . . . . Then in the fourth generation they will return here (Canaan), for the iniquity of the Amorite is not yet complete" (15:13-14, 16).

But for now, we're studying Jacob and his family as they live out their time in Goshen, the land given to them in Egypt.

What is God preparing you for while you are in your "Goshen"—the place of preparation as you wait to enter your "Canaan"?

Your "Goshen" experience may be as difficult as the Israelites', but view it as a time of equipping and preparation for what lies ahead in your "Canaan." Some of us may never walk a step in our Canaan until we step into eternity with Jesus, but all that happens to us here is preparing us for the life to come. Godliness is profitable for all things since it holds promise for the present life as well as for the life to come (1 Timothy 4:8b).

[1]Holman Old Testament Commentary: Genesis (Nashville: Broadman & Holman, 2002), 362.

Day Two

The Great Shepherd

The famine conditions play out just as Joseph's interpretation of Pharaoh's dream said they would. The Canaanites, as well as the Egyptians, were affected, which reminds me of the ancient proverb, "Desperate times call for desperate measures." Thankfully, there is a wise man in Egypt with a plan—Joseph!

Read Genesis 47:13-27. Name the three stages of Joseph's economic plan.

1) vv. 16-17

2) vv. 18-22

3) vv. 23-26

Whether the people agreed or disagreed with the policies Joseph set forward, they still believed in Joseph, so they were grateful and glad to do it, considering the alternative of starving to death (v. 25). Joseph became the distributor of all food supplies, which allowed the Egyptians and Joseph's family to live during the famine. Just as Pharaoh blessed Jacob and his family by giving them land and provision, God blessed Pharaoh by giving him land and affluence. In the Book of Exodus, when another Pharaoh arose who did not know Joseph or the blessings which Pharaoh had received through him (1:8), the Egyptians began to experience the curses that came upon those who cursed Abraham's descendants (Genesis 12:3).[1]

"And I will bless those who bless you,
And the one who curses you I will curse.
And in you all the families of the earth
will be blessed."
(Genesis 12:3 NASB)

Pharaoh is the title for an Egyptian king. Just as we have many Presidents in our country, so there were many different Pharaohs in the history of Egypt. They typically did not mention the name but only went by their respected name—Pharaoh. The Pharaoh ruling during the time Jacob and his family entered Egypt was Sesostris III. Another Pharaoh was in power at the time of Joseph's death, and he did not know Joseph.[2]

Joseph is similar to Christ in another way. Joseph was a great shepherd to his flock (family). He knew the best location for his flock to live and the best language for his brothers to speak to Pharaoh, and he provided for them throughout the days of the famine. Joseph put his life on the line for his family when he went before Pharaoh to ask for provision for his family.

What do the following Scriptures reveal about our Good Shepherd?

John 10:11-18, 27

1 Peter 5:3-4

Revelation 7:16-17

A good and respectable shepherd would not forsake his flock but would gather them together to love, provide for, and care for them. By the words of John 10:27, we see Joseph was one of God's sheep who heard His voice. God knew Joseph, and Joseph obeyed Him in all that He asked him to do. Joseph had a personal relationship with God, which let him hear God's voice, and his response was to follow Him. What about you? Do you have an intimate relationship with your Good Shepherd? Does God know your voice? It involves two-way communication—one of listening and one of responding. Bob Sorge says, "Things don't change when you talk to God; things change when God talks to you."[3]

> *"Things don't change when you talk to God; things change when God talks to you."*
>
> ~ Bob Sorge

Is God impressing on your heart to make a change in your quiet time with Him? If so, what?

God is always right there to hear from us. It doesn't matter if you have missed a day in the Word, and that day has turned into a week, maybe a month, or even a year. God doesn't move, so return to Him and live (Amos 5:4).

Finish out the day with this final reading from Genesis 47:27-31.

What happened to Israel while they lived in Goshen?

Circle the amount of years Israel (Jacob) lived in the land of Egypt?

5 10 15 17 22

What was Jacob's request? To whom was the request given?

How was the request confirmed (v. 29)?

Jacob's actions in this portion of Scripture most assuredly demonstrates Joseph's superiority over his brothers. The private setting Jacob and Joseph enjoyed was one of intimacy. The request for Joseph to put his hand under his father's thigh is similar to today's courtroom custom of being sworn in on a Bible. In the ancient patriarchal world, the placing of a hand under a thigh close to the circumcised male sex organ connected the oath to the divine presence. For Abraham and his descendants, circumcision was a constant reminder of God's presence.[4]

Trusting Joseph with his life, Jacob called his son. Joseph responded very carefully at his father's bedside, promising to do all that he was asked. Once again, Joseph, a man of great character, followed through with his father's wishes—not just to be respectful, but to fulfill the promise by God to Jacob, Isaac, and Abraham so that his descendants could acquire the land of promise, Canaan. Joseph acted out his faith. Indeed, he gave life to his good intentions.

In today's fast-paced life, do we follow through with good intentions? It takes time, commitment, and your word. I have watched a friend care for her widowed mother with grace and love. Even five years after her father's home-going, she visits her mother every day, cares for her, and makes sure her needs are met. Others periodically come to her aid, but due to distance and time, it is difficult. To me, this is an act of love, respect, and heroism.

Give life to your good intentions.

To what or whom may God be asking you to renew your commitment? What is He asking of you? And will you set the time aside to mail that letter, wash someone's windows, relieve a friend of her duties for a day, make a meal, visit a shut-in, or just sit at a loved one's bedside for comfort?

What is God asking you to do as a result of today's study?

[1]Holman Old Testament Commentary: Genesis (Nashville: Broadman & Holman, 2002), 362.
[2]The Ryrie Study Bible (NASB) (Chicago: The Moody Bible Institute, 1995), 91.
[3]Bob Sorge, Secrets of the Secret Place: Keys to Igniting Your Personal Time with God (Lee's Summit, MO: Oasis House, 2005), 11.
[4]Holman Old Testament Commentary, 365.

Day Three

Lasting Legacy

We now come upon the second bedside scene of Joseph and Jacob. Little did Joseph realize the blessing that would come from his visit with his sons and their grandfather.

Read Genesis 48:1-5.

Who did Joseph take with him to visit his sick father?

What was their birth order (41:51-52)?

What was Jacob's response to the arrival of his son, Joseph?

What transpired in verse 5?

Isn't it true that when we set out to be a blessing to someone, we receive a greater blessing from our time shared with them? That is exactly what happened as Joseph visited his father with his two sons. And Jacob collected himself and sat up in bed (48:2).

A few years ago, my ninety-two-year-old grandmother, Jessie, became very ill. After a call from my mother, I decided I needed to make a trip to her bedside in the nursing/rehabilitation home where she was living in Florida. All I can remember as I flew down was my prayer asking God to spare her life until I arrived. I wondered what I would say to her.

On my way to the nursing home, I stopped by a Christian bookstore and purchased a devotional by an author she was familiar with—Billy Graham. Upon my first visit with her, my mother and I went in together as she lay in her bed. We exchanged kisses, but I knew I could not stay long since it was late and I just wanted to be able to see her.

As I awakened the next morning with much emotion flooding my soul, I went for a daily visit by myself. When I arrived at the rehabilitation center, much to my surprise, she was at therapy. Therapy, I thought. Wow, she is doing so much better. The nurses were just as shocked as I was. They shared with me how there was such a difference in her after I arrived. My mother concurred. She said, "I think she was waiting for you to arrive. You gave her a reason to live."

As we shared stories with each other, I asked her if I could read her the first devotion in her new book. She agreed. The first day was entitled, "Namesake." I am named after my grandmother, and I have always felt so honored with that. I don't remember all the details of the devotion—only that it asked what was behind a name. I was able to share the honor I felt to carry her name, ever since I was a little girl, along with the love I had for her. It was one of the sweetest moments of my life, one I will cherish for a lifetime. But honestly, it was the words she shared with me that made the trip worth the blessing.

Please share a blessed story with your group.

What does James 1:27 say is our responsibility?

Jacob repeated the Abrahamic covenant that he received many years earlier at Bethel, when he had a dream: "And behold a ladder was set on the earth with its top reaching to heaven . . . . And behold the Lord stood above it and said, 'I am the Lord, the God of your father Abraham, and the God of Isaac; the land on which you lie, I will give it to you and to your descendants" (28:12-13). But in this repetition of the covenant we read today, numerous descendants, as well as land, are emphasized. It is in this context that Jacob adopted Joseph's two sons as his own. This would guarantee a separate inheritance in the land for them that would equal the ones for the other eleven sons (48:5).[1]

Jacob's legacy to his sons arose from his desire that the promise of God not be forgotten in the future generations to come.

What legacy do you want to leave?

What are you doing in this season of your life that will last beyond your years?

When that same grandmother turned ninety years old, I was asked to give a speech regarding her life. In front of fifty-plus people, I shared about her lasting legacy. It wasn't the money she would leave or the gifts she would distribute that would endure throughout the generations, but her love for family and her perseverance despite the multiple deaths of two husbands, a daughter, an adult grandchild, and son-in-laws. It was her desire to live life to the fullest, which meant caring for those under her influence. Isn't that our desire, to make a mark on those who come behind us, a spiritual watermark that never fades away?

As I began working again today, a piece of paper in my handwriting fell on my desk. I'm not quite sure where it appeared from, but God knew it was what I needed to read. I believe it was from a podcast I listened to by Chip Ingram, but I'm not certain: "Leave them something that money can't buy." In other words, teach them to suffer well and show them how to work unto the Lord, manage their finances, make wise decisions, and live grace-filled lives. Now, that is an inheritance.

Isn't that our desire, to make a mark on those who come behind us, a spiritual watermark that never fades away?

Continue reading Genesis 48:6-22.

What do you believe hindered Jacob from recognizing Joseph's sons (vv. 9-10)?

Explain who received the "right-hand" blessing from Jacob, why Joseph was upset, and why Jacob insisted on the switching of the birth rank.

Whew! That was a lot at one time, wasn't it? If we looked back through the history of Genesis, we'd discover that the birthright-switch game is nothing new. The birthright of Ishmael was given to Isaac (17:19), Esau's to Jacob (27), his brothers' to Joseph (1 Chronicles 5:1), and now Manasseh's to Ephraim. At the beginning of Joseph's story, Jacob designated Joseph as his heir by endowing him with a foretaste of wealth—an extravagant coat. That meant, according to Hebrew tradition (and the Law, after Moses), that he would receive a double share of his father's estate. Now, at the end of the story, Jacob makes good on that pledge. He adopted Joseph's two sons as his own and gave them each one share of the estate. Through his sons, Joseph's piece of the inheritance is, as planned, a double portion.[2]

But this time the attempt to subvert the birth order is not by mistake or deception. Jacob was very adamant about what he was doing. They would both be blessed, just as Jacob received the promise, "Your descendants shall also be like the dust of the earth" (28:14). He was passing it on to Ephraim and Manasseh, but Ephraim, the younger grandson, would be greater (48:19).

What promise was passed on to Joseph (vv. 21-22)?

Using the name Israel, Jacob declared that he was about to die, but he believed God would be with Joseph and take his bones back to the Promised Land. Like Jacob, Joseph would return to the land after his death along with the nation of Israel over four hundred years later (Exodus 13:19).

Joseph had lived faithfully and was worthy of much blessing. Jacob did not miss this opportunity to recognize the superior character of his son in a tangible way—with a double blessing.

[1]Holman Old Testament Commentary: Genesis (Nashville: Broadman & Holman, 2002), 370.
[2]Walk Thru the Bible; Joseph: The Power of Forgiveness (Grand Rapids, MI: Baker Publishing Company), 67.

Day Four

Blessings Come Through Holiness

There are only two chapters left for us to study in this first book of the Bible—Genesis—the beginning of history and the foundation upon which all the books of the Old Testament and New Testament stand. When this study is complete, I encourage you to continue your reading of the Old Testament with the Book of Exodus.

Today's reading is lengthy, but please take the time to read through Genesis 49, the third bedside scene of Jacob, in one sitting. This chapter could take up weeks of study, so we will only address the blessing of a few sons today. Chapter 49 functions as a character document for the tribes of Israel. Jacob blesses each one of his twelve sons with descriptions of their individual character and sketches the principal outlines of their future. Hang in there; we are only one day from the finish.

Re-read Genesis 49:3-4.

Describe what Jacob means by "turbulent as the waters" (NIV) or "uncontrolled as water" (NASB) in his blessing/prediction for Reuben.

Uncontrolled as water literally means "a boiling over of water," a vivid illustration of instability. No prophet, judge, or hero came from this tribe.[1]

Read Matthew 6:24 and James 1:6-8.

Explain how the terms, "turbulent" and "double-minded" are connected. What lessons do you learn from this?

Let your eyes look straight ahead;
fix your gaze directly before you.
Give careful thought to the paths for your feet
and be steadfast in all your ways.
Do not turn to the right or the left;
keep your foot from evil.

(Proverbs 4:25-27 NIV)

God is asking us to have a whole-hearted allegiance to Him and no one else. To do this, we must keep our eyes focused on Him alone and not turn to the right or the left (Proverbs 4:27). We can't afford to be like Reuben, who forsook his birthright and forfeited his place of preeminence because of his fornication with his father's maid servant, Bilhah (35:22).

Why do you think Simeon and Levi are linked together, according to Genesis 49:5-7? (Hint: look back at Genesis 34:24-31.)

The brothers are condemned for their cruelty and hot-tempered anger. In verse 6, Jacob disassociated himself from their evil motives and actions. From that point forward, they would be separated from each other, unable to be ringleaders who would cause others to sin. Levi's curse was later changed to become a means of blessing (Deuteronomy 33:8-11) because of the Levites' actions in Exodus 32:25-26 when Moses called, "Whoever is on the Lord's side, come to me!" All the sons of Levi gathered together to him.

What does Romans 13:12-14 say about change?

Ladies, thankfully there is room for change. Just as you are, in Jesus, you can lay aside your old self, which is being corrupted in accordance with lust and deceit, and be renewed in the Spirit. Put on the new self that is developed in the likeness of God (Ephesians 4:21-24). You have been created anew, so put on Jesus (Romans 13:14)!

The last two brothers left that we will study today are Judah and Joseph. Continue reading Genesis 49:8-12 for Jacob's blessing and prediction over Judah.

From memory, list all that you remember about Judah from our study, even as far back as Genesis 38.

What does Judah's blessing reveal?

What does Judah's prophecy reveal?

The blessing of Jacob's fourth-born son, Judah, is the most theologically significant of all the blessings reiterated in this chapter. Judah's major trait was represented by a lion's cub, a picture of sovereignty, strength, and courage. Although Judah started down the wrong path with his family, he repented (38:26) and then showed leadership (43:3-10). Judah was declared to be the royal tribe and identified as the one through whom the future rulers, King David and the Messiah, would come.[2]

The scepter was a sign of royal command, so Judah was given the right to rule until Shiloh came (49:10). In the Hebrew, "Shiloh" (shiyloh)[3] refers to "tranquil," an adjective that epitomizes the Messiah. Genesis 49:10b-12 describes the conditions that would occur once the Messiah ruled. Yet, as for Judah, he would be strong and powerful among the Israelites.

Read Revelation 5:5.

What tribe does Jesus comes from?

I want to take a slight detour into the lineage of Jesus, starting with Judah and Tamar.

Read Matthew 1:1-16. List the names of the four women mentioned in the lineage of Jesus.

v. 3

v. 5

v. 6

v. 16

We can trace Jesus's lineage back to Tamar, the woman who deceived Judah. Tamar, a Canaanite woman; Judah, a Jew. This is regarded by Bible commentators as foreshadowing of the reality that both Jews and Gentiles would share in the blessing of the Gospel.[4]

What is the secret (mystery) that is revealed and to whom, according to Colossians 1:26-27?

Hang in there; there's only one brother left. This is the most important one, the reflection of all our weeks of study. Re-read Genesis 49:22-26 for the blessing and prophecy of Joseph.

According to verse 22, how is Joseph described?

According to verses 23-24, who do you think the "archers" (attackers) refer to? And where did Joseph gain his strength?

According to verse 26, what was the stipulation for Joseph to obtain his blessings?

Joseph was a fruitful man throughout his tumultuous life. He overflowed with grace and honor as he approached each trial. The phrase "whose branches run over the wall"

The blessings of your father
are mighty beyond the blessings of
my parents,
up to the bounties of the everlasting hills
May they be on the head of Joseph,
and on the brow of him who was
set apart *from his brothers.*
(Genesis 49:26 ESV emphasis mine)

(49:22) indicates the extent of Joseph's fruitfulness. The picture is that of a vine or tree whose growth is so healthy that its branches extend beyond the wall or fence or the field in which it is located. Joseph was like that, for he not only bore fruit in his home; but his branches also reached out beyond his home. They reached into Potiphar's home, then the prison, then Pharaoh's palace, and then into much of the world.[5]

For your last Scripture reading today, read 2 Corinthians 6:14-18 and explain what Paul calls you to.

"Joseph put holiness before happiness, purity before pleasure, and God before man." ~ John G. Butler

Separation is certainly unpopular in today's culture, but separation is still the way to blessing, as Joseph's life proves. Just as Joseph separated himself from his brothers in convictions, interests, and loyalties, so we must practice separation from certain places, people, practices, and philosophies through the way we live out our morals, marriages, businesses, and religious views.

Take a moment and write a prayer about your devotion to God and willingness to be sold out for Him. (If you are not at this place yet, tell Him and ask Him to put that desire in your heart.)

[1]The Ryrie Study Bible NASB (Chicago: The Moody Bible Institute, 1995), 83.
[2]Holman Old Testament Commentary: Genesis (Nashville: Broadman & Holman, 2002), 372.
[3]James Strong, The New Strong's Exhaustive Concordance (Nashville: Thomas Nelson Publishers, 1990), 115.
[4]Herbert Lockyer, All the Women of the Bible (Grand Rapids, Michigan: Zondervan, 1967), 163.
[5]John G. Butler, Joseph: The Patriarch of Character (Clinton, Iowa: Regular Baptist Press, 1993), 167.

DAY FIVE

Joseph: A Typology of Jesus

First, great job yesterday! I know it involved more work than the other days, so thank you for hanging in there with me. This journey together has been wonderful and an all-inspiring one, to say the least—watching a young man's walk through life. It's one of greatness, humility, loneliness, peril, and delight. It's hard for me to grasp this is our last day together. I have such deep compassion for each one of you, and you were forever on my mind as I wrote. You were at the forefront of each book read, Scripture look-up, and question asked. Yes, the days of writing can be long and sometimes lonely, but I never feel completely by myself. I would see faces of women as God prompted a question, read a quote, and typed words on the page. I pray this study of Joseph has caused you to draw closer to God, reach out to Jesus for comfort and draw from the power of the Holy Spirit for whatever situation you find yourself in during this season of your life.

This morning in my quiet time I read Deuteronomy 2:3, in which God spoke to Moses and said, "You have circled this mountain long enough. Now turn north." I don't know what you are facing today, but just like Moses discovered, today is a new day, and God may want you to stop circling that same mountain—that mountain of negative self-talk expressions such as "I am not good enough," or "I am not worthy enough." Or, you may be seeking the approval of man, feeling despair, or asking forgiveness of the same thing over and over again. Whatever may be causing you to go "around and around," it has been long enough. Turn north and head the other way. Arise and set forth (Deuteronomy 2:24).

How does this statement "You have circled this mountain long enough. Turn north" parallel the events in Joseph's life?

How does this same statement speak to you today?

> *"He brought us out from there in order to bring us in, to give us the land which He had sworn to our fathers."*
>
> (Deuteronomy 6:23 NASB)

There are some things we just have to change our mindset about. In Joseph's case, he circled a lot of the same situations, but he made the adjustments he needed to in his mind. He learned to turn away from certain people and turn to God instead. God took him in and out of difficulties to bring him into a better situation altogether.

Read Deuteronomy 6:23. Discuss what God may be bringing you out of in order to take you to a better place, situation, or relationship.

Today, we will approach not only the closing of Jacob's eyes, but those of our main man, Joseph, as well.

Read Genesis 49:28-33 and record the final hours of Jacob's life.

Jacob died when he was 147 years old (47:28). He went to Egypt when he was a hundred and thirty years old (v. 9); thus, he lived in Egypt for seventeen years. Jacob had two seventeen-year periods with Joseph. The first seventeen years of Joseph's life paralleled the last seventeen years with Jacob in Egypt, with days of joy, provision, honor, and mourning.

From memory, compare both of these periods of seventeen years of joy, provision, honor, and mourning from Jacob and Joseph's individual perspectives.

Joseph's first seventeen years under his father's protection:

The second seventeen years of Jacob's protection under Joseph:

What is Joseph's reaction to his father's death, according to Genesis 50:1-6?

The beginning of Joseph's life and his reunion with Jacob in Egypt were both joyous moments. Yet Joseph also experiences mourning—at the end of his first seventeen years due to the separation from his father, and at the end of the last seventeen-year period he shares with

Jacob in Egypt, when his father died, Jacob's death is observed in a very Egyptian manner, with a forty-day mummification and seventy days of mourning.

Continue reading Genesis 50:6-14. Who was present at the burial of Jacob? Where did they go?

Can you picture the entourage of people leaving Egypt to travel to Canaan? It included the servants of Pharaoh, the elders of his house, all the elders of Egypt, all the house of Joseph, his brothers, and his father's house, along with chariots and horsemen (50:7-9).

What a sight this must have been! This was such a tribute to Jacob, as they honored him with their presence. Much of Jacob's honor came from the way Joseph lived among the Egyptians, and so the Egyptians wanted to honor Joseph by paying their respects to his father.

Read Genesis 50:14-21 and answer the following questions.

Circle where the brothers remained after the burial of Jacob.

Canaan Egypt Mt. Sinai Ur Sodom

What did the brothers fear? How did they respond to their fear?

What was Joseph's response to their request—emotionally, verbally, and providentially?

Without the security of Jacob's presence, the brothers feared Joseph would take revenge against them and kill them. Perhaps they really never felt that Joseph fully forgave them. Nearly forty years had passed since they sold Joseph into slavery, and they still lived with the same regret because of their evil deed. Indeed, one may experience pleasure for a moment, but its lasting effect can be destructive throughout a lifetime if it's not brought into the light of Jesus Christ. What is God asking you to bring into His light for forgiveness?

While writing this study, I polled women and an overwhelming number said their favorite statement of Joseph was, "As for you, you meant evil against me, but God meant it for good in order to bring about this present result, to preserve many people alive" (50:20). This verse shows the deep love of God that ran through the veins of Joseph. There was no trace of vengeance or bitterness whatsoever in his heart. Humanly speaking, this attitude is unachievable, but when the Spirit of God lives within (withon) you, such an attitude can be and should be displayed to the glory of God.

One may experience pleasure for a moment, but its lasting effect can be destructive throughout a lifetime if it's not brought into the light of Jesus Christ.

Write out Romans 8:28.

Is there a situation in your own life that you should apply Genesis 50:20 and Romans 8:28 to? And what would it look like if you did?

Our last reading about Joseph's amazing life takes place in Genesis 50:23-26. Joseph was thirty-nine years old when Jacob moved to Egypt. His father lived for another seventeen years there. For the next fifty-four years, the only things about Joseph's life we know are that he stayed in Egypt, died at the age of one hundred and ten, and saw his grandchildren and great-grandchildren. We aren't told anything about these fifty-four silent years. Is it possible as a different Pharaoh came to power, Joseph's own influence faded as he aged? Maybe so, but his legacy still lived on. In fact, he has become an example to us as a trusted saint of the faith.

From all that you have studied about Joseph's life, what characteristic of Joseph do you most desire to portray? (If there are more than one, please share.)

What is the promise passed down to his brothers before Joseph's death in Genesis 50:24?

What was Joseph's last request before he died in Genesis 50:26?

Joseph's final words showed that he cared more about God than himself. When he said, "God will surely take care of you," he was directing their attention to the faithfulness of our Heavenly Father and the certainty of His Word. He declared what God said He was going to do, which He indeed did. Joseph's words, "You shall carry my bones up from here" (v. 25), was a reminder that Egypt would not be their permanent home. He was instilling within them Genesis 15:12-16, the promise given to Abraham: "Know for certain that your descendants will be strangers in a land that is not theirs, where they will be enslaved and oppressed four hundred years."

Now when the sun was going down, a deep sleep fell upon Abram; and behold, terror and great darkness fell upon him. God said to Abram, "Know for certain that your descendants will be strangers in a land that is not theirs, where they will be enslaved and oppressed four hundred years. But I will also judge the nation whom they will serve, and afterward they will come out with many possessions. As for you, you shall go to your fathers in peace; you will be buried at a good old age. Then in the fourth generation they will return here, for the iniquity of the Amorite is not yet complete."

(Genesis 15:12-16 NASB)

Look up Hebrews 11:22 and record what the great chapter of faith says about Joseph.

Oh, how I wish we could continue right into the Book of Exodus to see all that was predicted. Maybe that's for another study. However I do want us to close with a few extra Scriptures from Exodus and Joshua to see how this story pans out for Joseph (his bones).

Read the following Scriptures and record what is said about Joseph.

Exodus 1:8

Exodus 13:19

Joshua 24:32

Wow, Joseph was such a memorable man in the life of Egypt; but in Israel's history, he was forgotten. However he wasn't forgotten by those who mattered: Moses, Joshua, and all of Israel. It just goes to show how Joseph's legacy lived on for over four hundred years—throughout Israel's captivity, deliverance, and entrance back into Canaan. Joseph's life was one of purpose exemplified and faith rewarded, and the sovereignty of God won. The bones of Joseph served their purpose. They were a continual reminder of the faithfulness of God through the fulfillment of Joseph's dream in ways that reached far beyond what he could have ever imagined.

My dear sisters, thank you for journeying with me through the life of Joseph. I pray you not only learned much about the history of Israel, but also about our Lord and Savior through the similarities of Joseph's life with the life of Jesus. The story of Joseph certainly is a foretaste of the life of Jesus. Many parallels do exist: They both were sent on a mission from their fathers, rejected by their brothers, and sold for silver. In addition, they both suffered for the good of those who betrayed them, were found faithful through temptation, served as shepherds of their flocks, and offered forgiveness to those who did not deserve it. Indeed, Joseph is a typology of Christ.

Oh, that you would be an example to those around you as you live out a life of fruitful purpose in every step you take.

Typology - A type is an event, character, or institution which has a place and purpose in history but which by divine design can correspond to a later event, character, or institution (the antitype). The value of typology lies in recognizing that God has foreknowledge. He can design and record in a specific manner an earlier event, character, or institution to resemble a later one. This helps the reader of Scripture to see God's hand in all of history.[1]

Be a blessing,

Jessie

[1]Holman Old Testament Commentary: Genesis (Nashville: Broadman & Holman, 2002), 378.

WEEK SIX
VIDEO SESSION

PRINCIPLE 6:

TAKE CARE OF YOUR CHARACTER, AND GOD WILL TAKE CARE OF YOUR **REPUTATION**.

ORDER INFO

JOSEPH

For autographed books, bulk order discounts,
or to schedule speaking engagements, contact:

Jessie Seneca
jessie@jessieseneca.com
610.216.2730

To order any of Jessie's books, visit
www.MoreofHimMinistries.org

Also available from your favorite bookstore
Like us on Facebook

Fruitbearer Publishing, LLC
302.856.6649 • FAX 302.856.7742
info@fruitbearer.com
www.fruitbearer.com
P.O. Box 777, Georgetown, DE 19947

Did you know that God has a secret? One day, while Jessie Seneca was reading Colossians 1:27 in the New Living Translation (NLT), she saw it. There it was, God's secret: "Christ lives in you. This gives you assurance of sharing in His glory." Once you know it, you will never be the same. You can enter into a wholehearted relationship with the supreme and all-sufficient Christ. This study features five weeks of personal, daily assignments and six weekly group sessions with DVD (available separately). As this study guides you into a deeper relationship with your heavenly Father and Savior, Jesus Christ, you will be grounded in the truth of Christ, the person of Christ, and the power of Christ. You will be challenged in your everyday relationships—in the home, workplace, and church. Read and study the short yet compelling and powerful letter of Colossians. When you are finished studying it, you will not only want to learn the secret for yourself, but live it out and pass it on.

A companion DVD and audio CD are available for this title.

Are you "living life" and wondering where all your plans went, only to realize that God's plans were always your plans and you just didn't see it? Road Trip is Jessie's journey in her battle with Cushing's Syndrome, a life-threatening disease. Her story looks back at her ride through the ups and downs of her struggles, how God brought her through them victoriously, and how He is using her experiences for His purposes. This book encourages you to see God's big picture in your own life and appreciate the detours and pit stops along the way that will help make you stronger and live a more purpose-filled life.

Includes a study guide for personal reflection or group discussion.

Made in the
USA
Middletown, DE